Best Ever Kids Costumes

KT-142-304

Best Ever Kids Costumes

Vinilla Burnham

COLLINS & BROWN

This book is dedicated to my nieces and nephew, Polly and Phoebe d'Abo and Ben and Amy Burnham.

First published in the United Kingdom in 2009 by
Collins & Brown
10 Southcombe Street
London
W14 0RA

An imprint of Anova Books Company Ltd

Distributed in the United States and Canada by
Sterling Publishing Co, 387 Park Avenue South, New York,
NY 10016, USA

ISBN 978-1-84340-475-0

A CIP catalogue for this book is available from the British
Library.

10 9 8 7 6 5 4 3 2 1

Reproduction by Rival Colour Ltd, UK
Printed and bound by SNP Leefung, China

This book can be ordered direct from the publisher.
Contact the marketing department, but try your bookshop first.

www.anovabooks.com

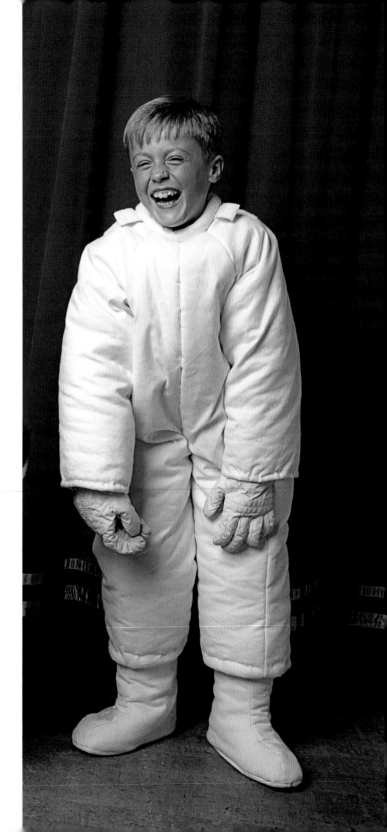

Contents

PROJECTS

Introduction

Kids love dressing up! It gives them a chance to make up and act out stories and, as every parent and teacher knows, stimulates their imagination through play.

This book contains 20 imaginative step-by-step costumes, ranging from a delicate, ethereal fairy to a ferocious, fiery dragon, a fluffy, cuddly bunny to a spooky, spiky Martian. The accompanying CD contains all the patterns you need, in a range of sizes to suit different ages.

The step-by-step instructions explain exactly how to make the costumes, using basic dressmaking techniques as well as more unusual methods that are used by professional costume makers in the theatre, film and television industries. These include making masks in foam, making wings, and 'distressing' and dyeing cosumes to make them look 'lived in', as if the character has a past. There are also some special costume effects that have been invented especially for this book, such as the foam 'nodules' on the Martian costume on page 59 and the mermaid scales for the Mermaid on page 133.

I have tried to incorporate materials that are readily available in craft and art shops as well as in general household and hardware suppliers. I've also given suggestions for buying materials and clothing such as second-hand dance wear and embellishments inexpensively on Internet auction sites. Throughout the book, you'll find a wealth of useful tips and shortcuts for those of you who are short of time.

My hope is that this book will inspire and encourage the whole family to get involved. Costume making can be a great introduction to creative craft and design skills for children, as they can help to choose materials and colours; it's their costume after all, so their opinion matters! And even if they're too young to wield a pair of scissors or a needle and thread, they can help to colour things in or stick on sparkly beads. Grandmothers with craft and sewing experience – and perhaps a little more time on their hands than busy young mums – can help with the time-consuming elements such as sewing on sequins and scales. Dads and uncles with DIY, mechanical and model-making skills will love to help make projects such as the Space Man (page 50) or the foam head of creatures such as the Fiery Dragon on page 106.

I've given suggestions for fabric colours and accessories, but of course the final choice is yours. Feel free to adapt and decorate the costumes in any way you choose. You could, for example, transform the Dragon on page 106 into a dinosaur, simply by changing the colour and making different sizes and shapes of spines – or, if you leave off the mane and choose a patterned fabric, the Lion on page 36 could become a leopard or a tiger.

Whether you're making a costume for a special birthday party, a fancy-dress competition, for your little ones to go 'trick or treating' in, or for a school play, I hope that you'll have as much fun making them as your kids will have wearing them!

Vinilla Burnham

Getting started

At the beginning of each project in this book, you will find a list of all the tools and materials that you will need. There are, however, lots of general bits of equipment that you will use time and time again.

Equipment

There are certain basic tools that you will need but, except for a sewing machine, they are not too expensive. You will probably already have most of the sewing equipment that you need. Good-quality scissors are essential and you will need several kinds – paper scissors for cutting out the patterns, fabric scissors, pinking shears and small, sharp scissors for snipping thread, clipping into seam allowance and detailed work. You will also need pins, safety pins, a tape measure and needles in various sizes for hand stitching. Finally, equip yourself with a range of marking tools – tailor's chalk, dressmaker's carbon paper and a tracing wheel, and marker pens – to cope with different types of fabric.

You will also need some general crafting equipment. A craft knife and cutting mat are useful for cutting through foam and other substances, although they are quite expensive; a rubber mat, polyboard or even a couple of layers of thick cardboard taped together make inexpensive alternatives.

You will also need glues to suit different materials (check the manufacturer's instructions to find out what type is suitable for the material you are using and how to apply the glue). When using contact adhesive, always wear a face mask and disposable plastic gloves, and work in a well-ventilated area.

A tagging gun (available from shop outfitters in micro, fine and standard sizes) is a really speedy way of attaching trims, and well worth investing in if you're going to be doing a lot of costume-making. However, these guns have extremely sharp needles and must be used with extreme caution. No child should ever be allowed to handle the gun.

Using the CD

The CD supplied with this book has all the patterns needed. It uses PatternMaker's Pattern Viewer to print them out. You will need either a PC, PC laptop or an Intel-based Mac to run it. For Windows, you will need any of 98/NT/2000/ME/XP/Vista. For an Intel-based Mac you will need some form of Windows or a Windows Simulator such as CrossOver Mac (PatternMaker is Silver Certified and a free 30 day demo copy is included on the disc – see PDF manual on the CD for instructions on how to get patterns in .pdf form to keep), Leopard (requires a copy of Windows), BootCamp (requires a copy of Windows), Parallels (requires a copy of Windows) and VMWare Fusion (requires a copy of Windows). The program requires 150 MB of disc space and to get full functionality you will also need Adobe Reader and Adobe Flash Player. These are both also included on the disc.

For a PC installation the disc should start straight away but if it doesn't navigate to your CD drive and click on index.htm. You will be able to install the program from that page by clicking on the link that says 'Install PatternMaker Software'. If asked, you will want to allow the ActiveX control. (This is a security feature to prevent you from installing something without your knowledge.)

Once the installation has started, you will be able to set your measurement units – either centimeters or inches, and the program will ask you for a password. **The password is 2CoSTuMeS2**. Type in the password exactly as it is shown here as it is case sensitive. Please keep your book and disc together as you will need both to re-install your software and PatternMaker is not able to issue the password again. All the files you need to operate PatternMaker are included on the disc and are also placed in your Start Menu. Please read the section in the PDF manual on 'How to run a macro'.

Intel-based Mac Installation requires a little help. Your Mac will need to be prepared to run PatternMaker first. A Mac that has a legal copy of Windows will result in the program running in Windows, so all of the navigation, keyboard shortcuts, etc., will remain as they are listed in the manual. Complete instructions for using CrossOver Mac are included in the PDF Manual under 'PatternMaker on a Mac'. Simply navigate to your PatternMaker CD and then index.htm to view it.

Be sure to check the CD tips page on the disc as well as the website mentioned in the 'How to update' section in the PDF manual to see if there has been an updated version of PatternMaker.

Printing the patterns

The CD contains all the patterns you will need to make the projects in this book. Just select the size of the child for whom you are making the costume and print out the pieces at the correct size. There are instructions in the PDF manual for a child who is between sizes. You will probably need to paste several sheets of paper together to get the full pattern. After you have selected your pattern and the size you need, the pattern pieces required will appear as outlines on the screen. You can move these outlines around on the screen before printing them out, so that each one is made up of as few pieces of paper as possible. Each sheet will have matching points printed on each corner. Just line these up and tape the sheets together to get your pattern pieces, then cut out each pattern piece roughly before pinning it to the fabric.

Cutting layout and fabric amounts

The program allows you to type in the width of the fabric you want to use and then lay out the pattern pieces on screen to fit them into a length of fabric. Note that some pieces need to be placed to a fold line along one edge; this is noted on the pattern piece itself. When you are happy with your layout, you can print it out to follow when pinning the pieces to the fabric. The box at the top of the screen will also tell you how much fabric you need to buy for your layout.

Techniques

Tacking stitch

This is a technique used to temporarily hold layers of fabric together for fitting or to prevent slipping as seams are stitched. It is traditionally done with large, single-thread stitches and is removed after the final sewing has been completed. Knot one end of the thread and work a long running stitch through all the layers of fabric.

Slipstitch

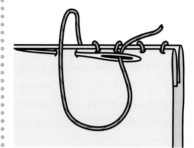

This stitch is usually used to join folded edges, which should be almost invisible. Lay the pieces one on top of the other, folded edge to folded edge, and bring the needle through the folded edge of the bottom piece from the back so the knotted end is secured inside the fold. Take a tiny stitch through the edge of the top fold, then go back into the top layer of the bottom piece of fabric and slide the needle a little way along inside the fold to come out again on the edge. Continue in this way until the seam is complete.

Whipstitch

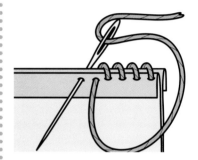

Whipstitch is used to join two edges together. Insert the needle from back to front, at right angles to the finished edges, to make a small, slightly slanted stitch. The stitches should be very close together and only as deep as necessary to create a firm seam.

Herringbone stitch

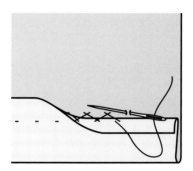

This is worked from left to right in a series of diagonal stitches up and down, crossing slightly at top and bottom. Secure the thread end in the folded hem, then take a long diagonal stitch and catch a few threads of the single layer of fabric in a tiny backstitch. Go back diagonally in the opposite direction and take a backstitch through the folded layer, but not through to the front surface. Repeat along the hem. There should only be a tiny stitch showing on the right side of the fabric. Herringbone stitch is useful for heavy or stretch fabrics, as the stitches are more flexible than in hemming and will give slightly.

Stab stitch

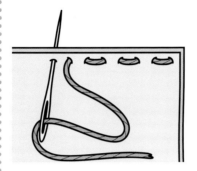

Holding the needle at right angles to the fabric, thrust the needle through the fabric, through all layers, and then bring it back again. You may find that it helps to wear a thimble.

Baseball stitch

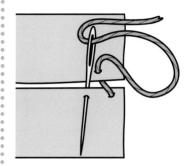

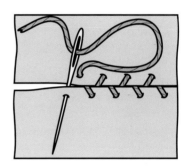

Baseball stitch is a decorative stitch that is used to join two abutted edges. Insert the needle between the edges, bring it out 1–2 mm (⅛ in.) from one edge, insert the needle between the edges again, and bring it out 1–2 mm (⅛ in.) further along. Work the stitches close together for a secure seam.

Flat seam

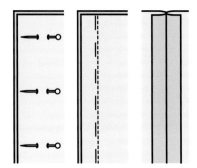

There are several kinds of seam used in dressmaking, but the projects in this book use only the very simplest – a flat seam.

Pin the pieces of fabric right sides together. You can either mark the seamline or use the guides engraved on the sewing machine footplate to achieve an even seam allowance. For complex seams or slippery fabrics, it may be safer to tack the pieces together by hand before stitching.

Sew the seam on the machine using a simple straight stitch with a short run of backstitching at each end to secure. Finally, remove the tacking threads and press the seam, either opened out flat or to one side, as instructed.

Clipping concave curves

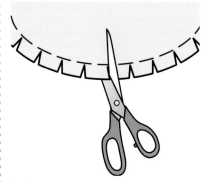

Make little clips or snips in the seam allowance just up to, but not through, the line of stitching, so that the seam will lie flat.

Clipping convex curves

Cut wedge-shaped notches from the seam allowance to eliminate excess fullness.

Inserting a zip

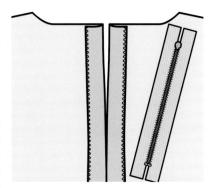

1 Mark the zip position on the seam, using the zip as a guide. Stitch the seam to the bottom mark, leaving enough room at the top for a facing seam. Zigzag stitch the raw edges.

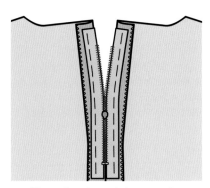

2 Place the closed zip over the seam on the wrong side and pin in place. Tack along both sides of the zip tape to hold it firmly in position while you work. Turn the garment to the right side.

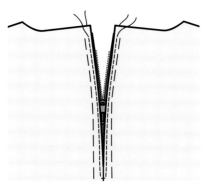

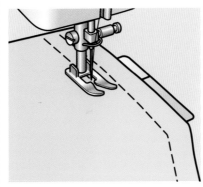

Gathering stitch

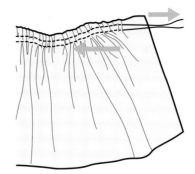

3 Using a zipper foot on the machine, start at the top and stitch down one side, across the bottom, and up to the top again to secure the zip in place. Move the zip slider if necessary to keep the seam straight, and keep the bottom corners nice and square.

1 Gathering using a machine stitch gives a more even result than hand gathering. Set the stitch length at its longest and loosen the tension slightly. Stitch once just inside the seamline, then again in a parallel line a very short distance away.

3 Pull both bobbin threads together at the untied end to gather up the fabric, easing the fabric along gently as you go. Adjust the gathers evenly along the required length, then fasten off the bobbin threads.

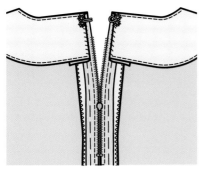

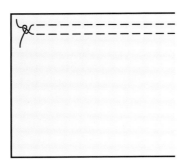

4 Add the facing or the waistband piece to the garment and slipstitch the ends to the zip tape. Make sure that no stitches or facings are likely to catch in the zip teeth in use. Remove any tacking and add any other fasteners required.

2 Tie the two top threads together on the right side of the fabric at one end, then tie the two bobbin threads together on the wrong side at the same end.

Ruching along the edge of a strip

Ruche the fabric along the straight edge by pushing the fabric tightly together in tiny pleats, using a large glass-headed pin, as it goes under the machine foot.

Ruching along the centre of a strip

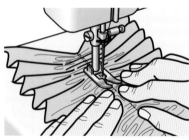

Push the fabric tightly under the macine foot with both hands. Run a second row of stitching over the first. Fold along the centre of the fabric and topstitch just in from the edge. It should now be possible to cut the ruched fabric into shorter lengths without the stitching coming undone.

Darts

1 Mark the dots indicating the line of the dart, or mark the entire stitching line if the dart has a curved stitching line, or if you prefer to do so.

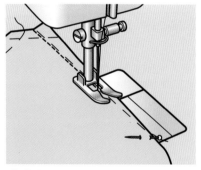

2 Fold the fabric in half, right sides together, along the centre line of the dart. Stitch from the seamline to the point of the dart, taking a couple of stitches beyond the point. Do not backstitch.

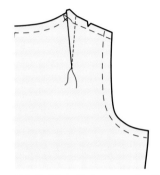

3 Finish with long ends, tie them together, then snip short.

Simple waistband

1 Transfer markings to the waistband sections. Add iron-on or sewn interfacing to the wrong side of one half of the waistband. Press the centre fold down the length of the waistband, right sides together.

Gathered set-in sleeve

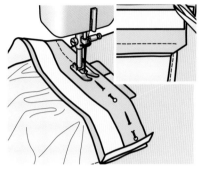

2 Pin or tack the waistband to the waistline of the garment with right sides together, notches matched, and the non-interfaced half next to the garment. Stitch the waistband seam, then stitch across the short ends of the waistband. Clip corners and trim seams.

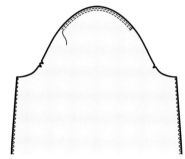

1 Make up the main sections of the garment. Transfer all markings to the sleeve pieces, then run a double line of gathering stitches between the dots at the sleeve cap. Zigzag the raw edges of the underarm seam.

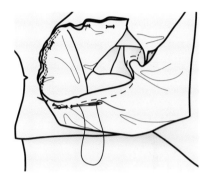

3 Tack the sleeve into the garment, making sure that the gathers over the top of the sleeve are even or the sleeve will look unbalanced. Stitch the sleeve into position.

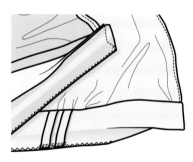

3 Finish the raw edge with zigzag stitching or by turning under and pressing. Turn the waistband right side out and pin or tack the inside layer in place. Topstitch just above the seamline on the right side.

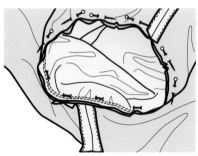

2 Stitch the underarm seam and press open. Turn the garment inside out. With right sides together, pin the sleeve into the armhole, matching seams and notches. Pull up the gathering threads to fit.

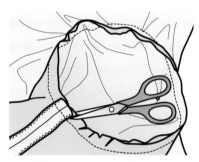

4 Clip the curve on either side of the underarm seam, being very careful not to cut through the stitching. Finish the raw seam edges of the armhole, either with zigzag stitching or binding.

Raglan sleeve

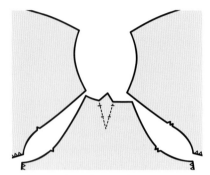

1 In a raglan sleeve, the seam runs from under the arm diagonally across to the neckline. Transfer all markings to the front, back, and sleeve pieces. Zigzag the raw side edges of all the pieces.

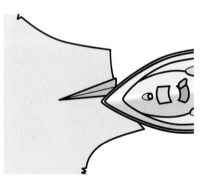

2 Some raglan sleeves have a dart at the cap for a better fit over the shoulder. Stitch the sleeve cap dart on each sleeve, then slash it open and press flat.

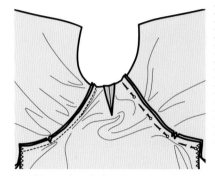

3 Pin and tack the sleeve to the front and the back, matching notches. Stitch together, then clip curves and press seams open.

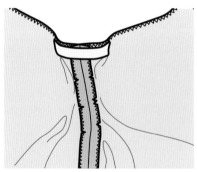

4 Pin and tack the sleeve seams, then stitch the sleeve/underarm seam. You can place a 10-cm (4-in.) length of tape across the seam to reinforce it.

Simple collar

1 Cut out the inside and outside collar pieces and the interlining. Iron the interlining to the back of one collar piece, making sure it is positioned within the seam allowance.

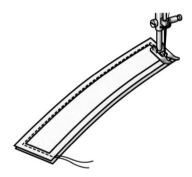

2 With right sides together, machine stitch the inside and outside collar pieces together along the top of the collar and both short ends.

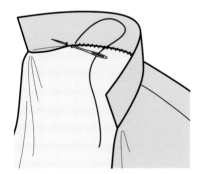

3 Clip the corners, turn right side out, and machine stitch the outside collar to the neckline of the garment.

4 Turn under the seam allowance on the inside of the collar and stitch the inside of the collar to the neckline of the garment.

Bias binding

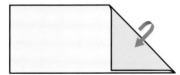

1 Fold the crosswise grain of the fabric to the lengthwise grain. The easiest way is to make sure the end of the length is straight on the grain then fold it down to line up with the selvedge.

2 Cut along the fold line, then take the triangle of fabric you have just removed and stitch it to the other end of the piece to make the parallelogram shape shown above.

3 Mark a series of lines parallel with the diagonal edge, twice the width of the binding apart. Number the bands 1, 2, 3, etc. down the left-hand edge with an air-erasable marker. On the right-hand edge, mark the end of band 1 as 2, then 3, 4, etc.

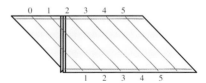

4 With right sides together, bring the edges round and match the numbers so 2 lines up with 2, 3 with 3, and so on. 1 and the last number will not match with anything. Stitch the seam with a 1-cm (½-in.) seam allowance, to create a tube of fabric. Press the seam open.

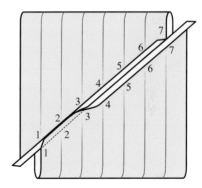

5 Cut along the marked line, which now runs around the tube in a continuous spiral. Fold both edges of the strip towards the middle and press in position, being careful not to stretch the bias binding as you work. A bias binding maker will make this process ea

Binding a straight edge

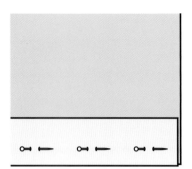

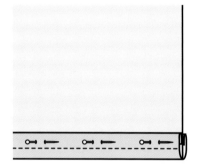

1 Open out the fold along one edge of the bias binding and place it right sides together on the edge to be bound, with raw edges matching. Pin in place, being careful not to stretch either edge.

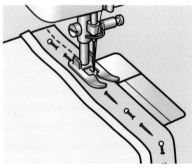

2 Straight stitch along the fold line of the bias binding, removing the pins as you work.

3 Fold the binding around the raw edges to the wrong side. If you don't want the binding to show, fold on the stitching line. If you want a narrow border of binding, fold on the centre line of the binding. Stitch along the folded edge on the wrong side, either hemming by hand if you don't want the stitches to show or with the machine.

Joining bias strips

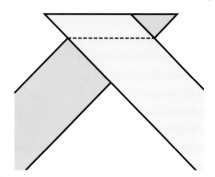

1 If you need to join two strips of bias binding, do it before you fold the edge over. Pin the strips right sides together, at right angles. Stitch together, leaving a 2.5-cm (1-in.) seam allowance.

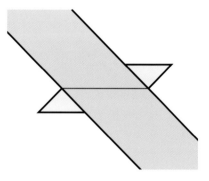

2 Press the seam open. Remember that if the bias strip has a pattern, you should try to match it to the seam line, not on the cut edges. Trim off the protruding points, and fold over the edges.

Piping and cording

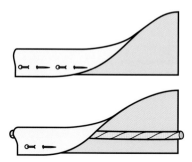

1 For piping, make a strip of bias binding twice the width you want the piping to be, plus 3 cm (1¼ in.) for the seam allowances. For cording, it should be three times the width of the cord, plus the seam allowances.

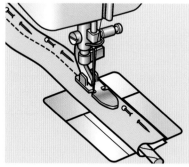

2 Fold the strip in half, wrong sides together and raw edges aligned. For cording, insert the cord into the fold and stitch along the strip as close to the cord as possible.

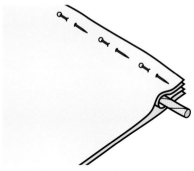

3 On the seam that is to be piped or corded, place the fabrics right sides together with the piping or cording in between and all raw edges aligned. Pin or tack together.

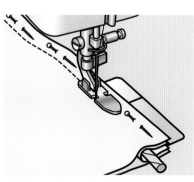

4 Use a zipper foot on your machine for cording; for piping you can just use the ordinary foot. Stitch along the seamline, being careful not to catch the cord in the seam as you work.

Using a tagging gun

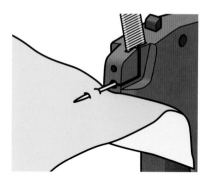

1 Pierce the needle of the gun carefully through the fabric and back again, as you would with a needle and thread, so that both ends are on the outside of the fabric.

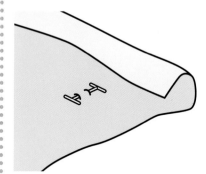

2 Click the gun to fire the tag through the material. Both T-bar ends of the tag will be on the outside of the fabric, so that they do not scratch the wearer. (See also page 8.)

Spats

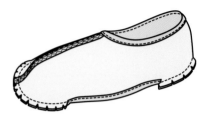

1 With right sides together, machine stitch the left and right spats together along the centre back and centre front seams. Trim the seams.

3 Machine stitch the toe cap in place, then cut notches into the curved seam.

5 Machine stitch around the ankle opening and hem.

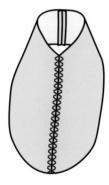

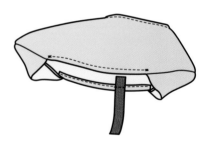

2 Zigzag stitch over the centre front seam, so that it lies flat.

4 Repeat to position the heel cap.

6 Turn the spat right side out and hand stitch an elastic stirrup in place to hold the spat in place over the shoe.

Balaclava and cowl

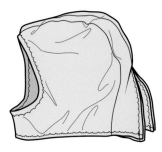

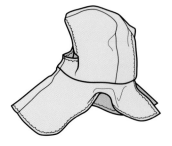

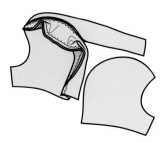

1 Cut out the balaclava side and centre panels and the cowl pieces (if required).

2 Tack or pin and, using a stretch stitch, stitch the centre panels for the inner and outer layers together separately, leaving openings in both centre backs for the Velcro fastening. Attach the side panels.

3 Place the inner and outer balaclavas right sides together, machine stitch around the face opening and turn right side out. Topstitch around the face opening by machine to keep the two layers together.

4 With right sides together, machine stitch the left and right sides of the cowl together. Stitch the two layers together around the outside edge and short sides. Turn right side out. Topstitch around outer edge, neck and centre back openings.

5 With right sides together, machine stitch the two layers of the cowl (if using) together around the outside edge and short sides. Turn right side out. Machine stitch the raw edge of the cowl onto the balaclava around the neckline.

6 Insert the Velcro fastening into the centre back seam.

Projects

With projects ranging from alien beings to soft, cuddly animals, and from a heavenly angel to a mischievous little devil, you're guaranteed to find costumes that suit your child's personality! Each project begins with a list of all the equipment and materials you will require, while the accompanying CD allows you to work out exactly how much fabric to buy. Detailed step-by-step instructions are given for each costume; read through them carefully, before you begin stitching, to make sure you understand them and have everything that you need.

shaggy sheep

This fluffy little sheep is just perfect for the stable scene in a school nativity play. Strips of muslin are gathered to form the 'fleece' – a process that is actually much less time-consuming than you might expect. The costume should be loose fitting, so err on the generous side when measuring.

You will need

**BODY SUIT
AND FLEECE COVERING**

White Lycra for body suit
Approx. 20 m (22 yd) natural muslin
    for fleece covering
White cotton quilted lining fabric,
    preferably with cotton on both sides
Black fleece for ears
Stiff iron-on interlining for ears
White zip to fit
4 x 2 cm (¾ in.) buttons

BALACLAVA

White Lycra
5 cm (2 in.) Velcro, 2 cm (¾ in.) wide
Approx. 50 cm (20 in.) fine white
    millinery elastic

HOOVES

Black Fun Foam or Funky Foam
Black elastic, 2 cm (¾ in.) wide, for
    stirrups
Pair of black gloves

GENERAL EQUIPMENT

Pins
Fabric scissors
Tape measure
Dressmaker's carbon paper and
    tracing wheel
Fine tagging gun and tags (optional)
Contact adhesive

Body suit and fleece covering

1 Cut out the body suit front, back and sleeves from white Lycra. Using dressmaker's carbon paper and a tracing wheel, mark horizontal lines at 4-cm (1½-in.) intervals, as indicated on the pattern, across the front and back of the body and each arm. (These lines show where to sew on the strips of fleece. You can sew them on by eye if you prefer, in which case you can omit marking out the lines.)

2 With right sides together, machine stitch the centre front and centre back seams, and insert the zip in the centre back seam (see page 12).

3 Cut the muslin across the width of the fabric into strips 15 cm (6 in.) wide. To speed things up, cut through several layers at once. (It does not matter if they are not perfectly cut.)

4 With the stitch length set to short-to-medium, ruche the fabric down the centre of each strip by pushing the fabric tightly together, using both hands, as it goes under the foot of the machine (see page 14). You can do this by eye, rather than marking out the centre line; some small discrepancies will not matter on this costume. If the strips do not look gathered enough, simply gather again on top of the existing ruching. Run a second row of stitching on top of the first for strength.

Speedy Shortcut

The fleece strips could be gathered by machining a double row of maximum-length stitching and pulling up the back threads, as in conventional gathering, but this method is much quicker.

shaggy sheep

5 Fold along the ruched line of each strip, and topstitch twice over this line with a medium-length stitch. You now have a double row.

6 Wash the strips by hand. This will shrink them, but will also make them crinkled and woolly, with loose threads and knots – just like a real fleece, the messier the better!

7 With right sides together, aligning the edges of the dart, pin and then machine stitch the dart at the top of the sleeve.

8 Set aside some strips to cover the balaclava. Using a wide zigzag stitch and following the marked-out lines, machine stitch the fleece strips onto the Lycra front, back and sleeves along the folded topstitched line, applying the ruched strips from the bottom up. Do not overstretch the Lycra or the costume may turn out the next size up. Continue the strips across any already joined seams, but stop at the seam allowance.

9 With right sides together, machine stitch the front to the back, along the shoulder, side and inside leg seams.

10 With right sides together, pin and machine stitch the underarm seams. Notch the curved shoulder seams. Repeat to make the second sleeve.

11 Turn the sleeves right side out. With right sides together, aligning the underarm seams with the side seams on the body suit, pin and machine stitch the sleeves to the suit.

12 If you are lining the body suit, cut out the body suit front, back and sleeves from quilted lining fabric. With right sides together, machine stitch the front to the back along the shoulder, side and inside leg seams. Turn right side out. Make up the sleeves in the same way as for the top fabric and set them into the lining suit (see page 15).

Speedy Shortcut

If you have a fine tagging gun, tag the strips of fleece to the suit at approx. 5-cm (2-in.) intervals (see page 19), instead of stitching them.

13 Cut out the tummy pads from quilted lining fabric. Slipstitch the pads to the lining of the suit, taking care not to stitch right through to the outside, to create the rounded tummy shape. Sew the two large pads (A) in first, both at the same time, and the two small pads (B) in on top of them.

14 Slot the quilted lining suit into the Lycra suit, wrong sides together. Turn in the seam allowances, then pin and slipstitch the two layers together around the cuffs, hems and neckline.

15 Sew the buttons to the outside of the sheep's neck, as indicated on the pattern. (These will correspond with elastic loops on the balaclava.)

Balaclava

1 Cut out the balaclava sides and centre panel from white Lycra. (You will need an inner and an outer layer.)

2 Using dressmaker's tracing paper and a tracing wheel, on the right side of the panels for the outer layer, mark lines to show you where to attach the strips of gathered muslin or tulle for the fleece, as indicated on the pattern. Also mark the seam lines. (You can mark the lines by eye if you feel confident enough.)

3 Tack or pin and, using a stretch stitch, stitch the centre panels for the inner and outer layers together separately, leaving openings in both centre backs for the Velcro fastenings.

4 Attach the side panels.

5 Make four elastic loops by taking short lengths of fine millinery elastic and knotting the two ends together. Machine or hand stitch the loops in place on the side panels, as indicated on the pattern.

6 Working one row at a time, starting from the bottom and working upwards, pin or tack the strips of ruched fabric in place along the marked lines on the outer balaclava, and then hand stitch or tag (see page 19) them in place. If possible, try to stitch through only the outer layer.

7 Insert the Velcro fastening into the centre back seam.

8 Fit the body suit and balaclava on the child. If there are any obvious gaps in the fleece, particularly around the face and neckline, fill them in with spare pieces of ruched fabric. It will be awkward to do this on the sewing machine at this stage, so use a fine tagging gun (see page 19) or hand stitch them.

Ears

1 Cut out four ear pieces from black fleece fabric and two from iron-on interlining. Following the manufacturer's instructions, iron the interlining to the backs of two of the ears. Note that the interlining stops short of the seam allowance; it should not get caught in the seam.

2 With right sides together, machine stitch each interlined piece to one of the non-interlined ears, leaving the bottom edge open. Notch the curved seams and turn right side out.

3 Hand stitch the ears onto the balaclava in a semi-circle, as indicated on the pattern, to create a rounded ear shape, with the interlined piece at the back of each ear.

Hooves

1 Cut out the hoof pieces from Fun Foam or Funky Foam.

2 If you are using Fun Foam, cut the fronts at an angle, as on the pattern. Using contact adhesive, glue the angled edges together, edge to edge. Glue the rest of the centre front and centre back seams together, edge to edge. Funky Foam can be zigzagged edge to edge or overlapped and topstitched on the sewing machine

3 Check that the opening is big enough for the child's foot. If it is not, trim away some of the foam. Sew or glue a black elastic stirrup under the instep. The hooves should be worn over rubber-soled soft shoes, such as neoprene diving-type shoes or simple gym shoes.

Finishing touches

1 Finally, go over every double row of muslin gathering on the costume and gently tease it apart. It tends to stick together after it has been washed; if it's fluffed up, it looks thicker and curlier. A pair of bought black gloves completes the costume.

Speedy Shortcut

Substitute black rubber-soled shoes for the hooves.

Fluttery Butterfly

Her gossamer wings decorated with shimmering spots of silk, this gorgeous little butterfly is guaranteed to set hearts a-flutter! The wings are formed from thin canes and are attached to the body by means of an elasticated harness, so they are lightweight and comfortable to wear.

You will need

DRESS

Silk chiffon or georgette for dress
Polyester georgette or Habotai silk for lining
Blue fabric dye, multi-purpose (hot) or cold
Salt
White leotard

WINGS AND HARNESS

Yellow Habotai or fine taffeta silk for wings
30 cm (12 in.) black Habotai or fine taffeta silk for appliqué
20 cm (8 in.) kingfisher blue Habotai or fine taffeta silk for appliqué
10 cm (4 in.) bright orange Habotai or fine taffeta silk for appliqué
Approx. 3 m (3¼ yd) fusible bonding web
6 mm and 3 mm cane, or 4 mm and 2 mm fibreglass rods (available from kite suppliers)

Approx. 60 cm (24 in.) white elastic, 7 or 8 cm (2¾ or 3 in.) wide, for waist strap
10-cm (4-in.) piece of Velcro, 5 cm (2 in.) wide, for harness waist strap
Approx. 1 m (1 yd) white elastic, 1 cm (½ in.) wide, for shoulder straps (optional)
Fine cable ties, black or white
2 or more fibreglass 'end stops' to fit the rods

ANTENNAE

Alice band with boppers
2 coloured furry or sparkly pipe cleaners (4 if very thin)
Coloured thread
Fuse wire (optional)

GENERAL EQUIPMENT

Pins, drawing pins
Tape measure
Fabric scissors
Pinking shears
Old large saucepan (for hot dye) or plastic bucket (for cold dye)
Old wooden spoon or tongs
Rubber gloves
Large piece of cork or soft board
Tracing paper
Black marker pen
Non-stick silicone baking paper
Contact adhesive
PVA adhesive
Hot or cold melt glue gun (optional)
Fine-nosed pliers
Masking tape
Wire cutters

Dress

1 If you are going to dye the hem (see Step 5), wash, dry and press the fabrics prior to making up.

2 Using pinking shears, cut out the front, back and side pieces from both the silk chiffon or georgette and the lining fabric. With right sides together, pin and tack the panels together as separate layers along the shoulder and side seams. Machine stitch the seams and press open, leaving openings between the back and side panels on both layers, as marked on the pattern, for the harness straps.

3 With right sides together, pin the lining over the top fabric and machine stitch around the neckline. Clip the curved seams and turn right side out.

4 Pin and tack the top and lining fabrics together around the armholes on the seam line. Trim the seam allowance of both fabrics to 2–3mm (1/8 in.) away from the seam line. Bind the armholes with a bias-cut strip of the dress fabric (see page 18).

5 Dyeing the hemline is optional. Mix the dye following the manufacturer's instructions. Test small pieces of fabric first to see how quickly the fabric absorbs the dye and to get the right shade (it looks darker when wet). Wet the dress to above the level of where you want to dip it to, then dip the hem into the dye. Quickly pull it out and dip again (and again) until you have the depth of colour you want. For a softer edge, do not hold the dress in the same position or you will get a hard band of colour.

6 Rinse the dress and hang it up to drip dry. Press the dress if you want a smooth finish; if you like a slightly crepey cheesecloth texture, which looks more organic, leave it as it is.

Useful Tip

The hem is likely to drop unevenly and both top and lining fabrics may react differently to the dye. I love this uneven look, but you will need to trim the hem if you want an even finish. Put the dress on the child, and measure up from the floor, marking the hem with pins. Trim the marked hem length.

Wings and harness

1 You will need a piece of cork or soft board big enough to easily fit one wing onto, with a margin of at least 6 cm (2½ in.) all around. Print out the wing plan pattern – preferably on tracing paper so that you can flip it from right to left.

2 Using drawing pins, attach the pattern to the board on the outer edges.

3 Lay the silk wing fabric over the pattern, making sure that the straight grain of the fabric lies across the line indicated on the pattern, from the shoulder point to the outer tip of the wing. (If it is not on the straight grain here, the wings will warp.) It is important that you can clearly see the pattern of the wing through the silk. If it is not clearly visible, draw over the lines on the pattern with a black permanent marker so that it shows through. Pin the silk around the edges of the board, using dressmaking or drawing pins.

4 Trace the wing pattern onto the silk wing fabric using a fine permanent marker pen.

5 Un-pin the silk and remove the printed pattern from underneath. Retain it for use on the second wing. Pin it to the wall for reference.

6 Now pin the fabric back on the board so that it is taut. Pin out any loose areas so that the tension is evenly distributed.

7 Following the manufacturer's instructions, apply fusible bonding web to the back of each appliqué fabric. Draw as many of the motifs as you can fit in on the paper backing of the bonding web. (Test your marker pen first, as the backing paper is resistant to some pens, while other pens just smudge.)

8 Cut out the motifs and remove the backing paper. Place the motifs in position, one by one, web side down, on the wing. Place a sheet of baking paper on top, then press with the iron to fuse the motif to the wing fabric.

9 Following the pattern, arrange the canes and/or rods one by one, on top of the silk wing fabric, to form the wing structure. Use 6-mm (1/4-in.) canes or 4-mm fibreglass rods for the main upright edges of each wing and 3-mm (1/8-in.) canes or 2-mm fibreglass rods for the 'veins' of the wings.

Working with Cane

Cane is normally supplied in tight coils. It is usually very flexible – unless it has dried out with age, in which case it can snap easily. Wet cane is much more pliable, but it will not stick if it is at all damp. If the cane needs straightening out, wet the cane and 'train' it into position by pinning it to the board. Angle pins on either side of the struts to keep them in place until dry. Please note that the type of cane that will work is called 'centre' cane. Bamboo or garden canes are not suitable for the wings.

For a stronger, more graphic look, dye or paint the canes using a large black permanent marker.

As an alternative to cane use fibreglass rod, which is available from most kite suppliers. This cannot be trained into a shape, but it can be flexed into the right curve following the lines on the pattern when bonded to the silk wing fabric with glue. Fibreglass rods may need to be cut using wire cutters. The dust from cut fibreglass can sting and itch and leave sharp shards at the cut ends so, if cutting is necessary, cover the cut ends with end stops or bind them with adhesive tape.

Speedy Shortcut

As a quicker, and less expensive, alternative to appliqué, you could paint the wing designs using fabric paints. Test the paints on your chosen fabrics first, and follow the manufacturer's instructions. The wings should be painted while the fabric is stretched in position on the board and must be fully dry before you apply the canes or fibreglass rods. Or, even speedier, choose a nice bright, single colour such as yellow or peacock blue.

10 Run a line of contact adhesive (see page 8) along one side of each cane or fibreglass rod. Run a 'snail trail' of adhesive along the corresponding lines drawn on the silk wing. Leave until the glue is touch dry, then firmly press the canes or rods onto the silk to bond.

11 Cut around the edges of the silk wing, leaving a 2-cm (³/₄-in.) margin to wrap around the main upright strut. If you have appliquéd or painted right up to the edge of the wing, the fabric should not fray; if there are any areas that might fray, run a fine line of clear or PVA adhesive round the raw edge.

12 Glue the cut edge of the fabric around the main upright strut and cut away any excess. The wing should now resemble a kite.

13 Repeat Steps 1–12 for the other wing, reversing the pattern to create a mirror image.

Harness

1 Following the pattern, using 6-mm (2¹/₄-in.) cane or garden canes cut to length, make up into a rectangle and affix cross struts by binding tightly with narrow strips of adhesive tape followed by a fine cable tie on all joints to secure. Garden canes, which are more

rigid, cheaper and readily available than centre cane, have a tendency to splinter, so bind them with tape and cover all cut ends.

2 If you are leaving the harness exposed, bind the canes with 1.5-cm (³/₄-in.) bias strips of the wing fabric, or with 1-cm- (¹/₂-in.)-wide cotton tape dyed yellow and glued at the ends. Alternatively, make a fabric covering for the harness using remnants of the wing fabric, folded over at the top and sewn at the sides like a simple chair-back cover.

3 Cut a length of 7- or 8-cm (2³/₄- or 3-in.) white elastic long enough to go around the child's waist, plus about 5 cm (2 in.) extra for an overlap. Stitch Velcro to the ends of the elastic as a fastening, making sure that the belt fits snugly but not too tightly around the child's waist. (If it is loose, the wings will wobble.) Wrap the elastic around the base of the side struts of the harness and sew in place, leaving an equal amount of elastic extending at each side. If necessary, make two shoulder straps to loop around the top corners of the harness and the child's shoulders, using 1-cm (¹/₂-in.) elastic.

4 To attach the wings to the harness, make tiny slits in the fabric right by the main struts of the wings – one at the top, one at the bottom and one in the middle of each strut. Slide a cable tie through each slit, and tie it around the main wing strut and the side strut of the harness with the cable end on the outside. Fasten tightly and cut off any excess.

5 To wear the wings, with the child wearing the leotard, thread the elastic waist straps though the openings in the seams at the back of the dress and fasten them (with the Velcro) on the inside of the dress. Check the correct position on the child so that the dress is not pulled or bunched up in any way.

useful Tip

To store, lie the wings flat, tape them to a wall with masking tape, or pin to a board. Do not rest the wings on the struts, or they may become distorted.

Antennae

1 Remove the springs from the head-bopper headband, leaving two stumps where the springs were attached.

2 If the pipe cleaners are too thin, tie two pipe cleaners together with a series of double or triple knots at about 2-cm (³/₄-in.) intervals, using coloured thread. Put a drop of PVA or all-purpose clear adhesive on each knot if you wish. Cut the threads close to the pipe cleaners, taking care not to cut the knots. Alternatively, you can use the pipe cleaners singly – but they will get bent more easily.

3 Using fine-nosed pliers, twist the top of each pipe cleaner (single or double) to form an even spiral at the top of the antennae. Bend the base of each pipe cleaner at right angles, about 1.5 cm (³/₄ in.) up from the base. Brace the angled section of pipe cleaner against the stump from the head boppers, with the end facing outwards.

4 Apply a small dab of PVA, all-purpose clear adhesive or hot or cool melt glue, then loop a piece of double thread or fine fuse wire around both the stump and the upright of the antennae, and bind round and round quickly and tightly before the glue sets. If they are correctly glued and bound with wire, the antennae should be firm and not wobble.

Shoes

Simple ballet flats are ideal for this costume.

Jewellery

Keep the jewellery simple. I used strings of tiny coloured lanterns made into a long necklace.

King of the Jungle

With his wild, tousled mane and long, swishing tail, this King of the Jungle will be a roaring success at any party gathering! Use face paints to add whiskers and other lion-like features, and buy or make a gold crown for a really regal finishing touch.

Lions have very flat fur, so a stretch velvet or fleece is a great choice of fabric for the body suit. These fabrics come in a wide range of colours and patterns, so you can easily adapt the design to make other animals, such as leopards and tigers.

You will need

MANE AND BODY SUIT

6 m (6½ yd) yellow dress net for sides of mane
6 m (6½ yd) brown dress net for centre of mane
'Lion-skin' fabric for body suit
White cotton quilted lining fabric, preferably with cotton on both sides (optional)
Chunky zip to fit
4 x 2-cm (¾-in.) buttons

BALACLAVA

Lycra in a similar colour to the body suit fabric
5 cm (2 in.) Velcro, 2 cm (¾ in.) wide
Approx. 50 cm (20 in.) fine black or white millinery elastic

EARS

Scraps of lion-skin fabric
Iron-on interlining

FEET

Scraps from body suit, or similar colour of felt
Black elastic, 2 cm (¾ in.) wide, for stirrups

TAIL

Small sheet 1-cm (½-in.) foam
20 cm (8 in.) lion-skin fabric from suit for covering
Plastic CD or DVD stack
Approx. 50 cm (20 in.) gathered brown net

GENERAL EQUIPMENT

Pins, safety pins
Fabric scissors
Tape measure
Tailor's chalk and/or marker pen
Dressmaker's tracing paper and tracing wheel
Fine tagging gun and tags (optional)
Contact adhesive
Curved needle (optional)

Mane

1 Fold the yellow and brown net fabric for the mane and tail in half lengthways and then in half again twice more, so that you have 16 layers.

2 Pin the layers of net together evenly. Once the net is pinned, you may find that the outside edges are uneven. Mark a straight line on the inside of the uneven edges and trim off anything beyond the line. (Dress net is inexpensive, so it doesn't matter if you waste a little.)

3 Using tailor's chalk or a marker pen (whichever shows up best on the net), mark and cut the fabric into strips 16 cm (6³/₄ in.) wide. (Depending on the quality of your scissors, you can cut through 20 or more layers of net at once as long as the layers are securely pinned together.)

4 With the stitch length set to short-to-medium, ruche the net down the centre of the strips by pushing the net tightly together as it goes under the sewing-machine foot (see page 14). If it isn't ruched tightly enough, repeat the process. Run a second line of machine stitching on top of the first, to stop it from unravelling when cut.

5 Fold each strip in half along the already ruched centre line and topstitch using a medium-length stitch. Cut through the strips of gathered net to the required lengths for the mane. You now have 'frillage' 8 cm (just over 3 in.) wide. Reserve one brown piece about 50 cm (20 in.) long for the tail.

Speedy Shortcut

Tagging, using a fine tagging gun, is a good alternative way to attach the net frillage (see page 19).

Useful Tips

If using the tagging gun, use it as if you are making stitches: go through the fabric, then back up again rather than just tagging straight through.

Make sure that both ends are on the outside, otherwise they will scratch the child's skin.

Be careful not to bend the needle, as they are expensive.

Body suit

1 Cut out the front, back and sleeves of the body suit from both the lion-skin fabric and quilted lining fabric.

2 Using dressmaker's tracing paper and a tracing wheel

and tracing over the pattern on the right side of the lion-skin fabric only, mark the lines where you will attach the strips of gathered net for the mane. Also mark the seam lines.

3 Working on a flat work surface, tack and then machine zigzag stitch the strips of gathered net one at a time to the individual lion-skin pieces, stopping at the seam lines. Start with the lowest rows first and work upwards. Tacking the net first will stop the fabric from stretching (or shrinking) and the net from sliding, so don't be tempted to skip this process; it doesn't take very long.

4 Pin, then tack the lion-skin fabric and the corresponding quilted lining pieces together. If your quilted lining fabric has cotton on only one side, then the two fabrics should be placed wrong sides together, so that the cotton side will be next to the child's skin.

5 With right sides together, machine stitch the two back pieces together, leaving an opening in the centre back for the zip as marked on the pattern. With right sides together, machine stitch the two front pieces together along the centre front. Insert the zip (see page 12).

6 With right sides together, machine stitch the front and back together along the shoulder, side and inside leg seams.

7 Bind the neckline (see page 18).

8 Cut out the pieces for the tummy pads from quilted lining fabric. Using herringbone stitch (see page 11) or slipstitch, stitch them to the inside of the suit to create the rounded tummy shape.

9 Turn the body suit right side out.

10 With right sides together, aligning the edges of the dart, pin and then machine stitch the dart at the top of the sleeve. With right sides together, pin and machine stitch the underarm seam. Clip the curved shoulder seam and press the seams open. Repeat to make the second sleeve.

11 Turn the sleeves right side out. With right sides together, aligning the underarm seams with the side seams on the body suit, pin and machine stitch the sleeves to the suit.

12 Sew the buttons to the outside of the lion's neck, as indicated on the pattern. (These will correspond with elastic loops on the balaclava.)

useful Tips

Remember that the mane changes colour, so check that you have the right colour of net on each panel. The pattern indicates which colour of net to use where.

Make sure that you make a right and a left side for the balaclava.

Balaclava (base for Lion's mane)

1 Cut out the balaclava pieces from Lycra. (You will need an inner and an outer layer.)

2 Using dressmaker's tracing paper and a tracing wheel, on the right side of the panels for the outer layer, mark lines to show you where to attach the strips of gathered net for the mane, as indicated on the pattern. Also mark the seam lines. (You can mark the lines by eye if you feel confident enough.)

3 Tack or pin and, using a stretch stitch, stitch the centre panels for the inner and outer layers together separately, leaving openings in both centre backs for the Velcro fastenings.

4 Attach the side panels.

5 Make four elastic loops by taking short lengths of fine millinery elastic and knotting the two ends together. Machine or hand stitch the loops in place on the side panels, as indicated on the pattern. These loops will hook around the buttons on the body suit to keep the mane attached.

6 Working one row at a time, starting from the bottom and working upwards, pin or tack the strips of ruched net in place along the marked lines on the outer balaclava, and then hand stitch or tag (see page 19) them in place. If possible, try to stitch through only the outer layer.

7 Insert the Velcro fastening into the centre back seam.

8 Dress the child in the body suit, then get him to try on the balaclava. If there are any obvious gaps in the mane, particularly around the face and neckline, fill them in with spare pieces of ruched net. It will be awkward to do this on the sewing machine at this stage, so use a fine tagging gun (see page 19) or hand stitch them.

Ears

1 Cut out four ear pieces from lion-skin fabric and two smaller pieces from iron-on interlining. Following the manufacturer's instructions, iron the interlining to the wrong side of two of the ears. Note that the interlining stops short of the seam allowance; it should not get caught in the seam.

2 With right sides together, machine stitch each interlined piece to a non-interlined piece, leaving the bottom edge open. Notch the curved seams, particularly right at the point, and turn right side out.

3 Hand stitch the ears onto the balaclava in a semi-circle, as indicated on the pattern, to create a rounded ear shape.

Feet

1 Cut the spat 'uppers' from a matching colour of felt.

2 Machine stitch the pieces together (see page 20) and attach elastic stirrups to the sides, checking the correct length first on the child.

Useful Tips

Do not put a continuous strip of net around the face; leave some small gaps to retain some stretch in the Lycra.

Do not let any net go over the edge and onto the skin or it will be very irritating.

Speedy Shortcut

Brown furry slippers make a good alternative to the spats.

Haircut

Try the costume on the child and assess the proportions. If the mane is too big, it will look like a buffalo! Trim it if necessary.

Tail

1 Cut out the tail from 1-cm (½-in.) foam.

2 Using contact adhesive (see page 8), glue the long edges of the foam tail together edge to edge to make a long, narrow cone.

3 Cut out the fabric for the tail covering. With right sides together, using a stretch stitch, machine stitch along the long edge to make another long, narrow cone. Turn right side out and feed the cover over the foam tail, aligning both seams at the back.

4 Check that the tail is not long enough to be trodden on by other children. If it looks too long, cut it down at the base.

5 Roll back about 5 cm (2 in.) of the fabric covering at the base of the tail to keep it clear of any glue. Cut down the base of a plastic CD or DVD stack to 7.5 cm (3 in.) in diameter. Apply contact adhesive to the upright central column of the stack. While the glue is still pliable, push the central column into the open end of the foam tail, so that the base of the CD stack is flush with the end of the foam tail. Leave to dry.

6 Stretch the fabric covering around the plastic base. Hand stitch across the base from top to bottom and then from side to side to form a web, pulling in the fabric to form a smooth base to the tail. (Imagine that you are lacing up a corset, but in a circle.)

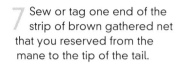

7 Sew or tag one end of the strip of brown gathered net that you reserved from the mane to the tip of the tail.

8 Spiral the net around the tip of the tail for about 10 cm (4 in.), securing it with a few hand stitches or tags at regular intervals.

9 Slipstitch the base of the tail to the body suit at the centre back seam below the waist, making sure you position it high enough for the child to be able to sit down without sitting on the tail. (The tail can be flicked to one side before sitting.)

Easter Bunny

This cuddly-looking Easter Bunny sports a lavish Easter bonnet overflowing with carrots, radishes and tasty greenery.

You will need

BUNNY SUIT, TAIL AND POM-POMS

Dark grey or brown fleece for bunny suit
Cotton quilted lining fabric, preferably with cotton on both sides, or calico or cotton drill
Strong zip to fit
Approx. 1 m (1 yd) elastic, 1.5-cm ($^3/_4$-in.) wide, for wrists and cuffs
Pale grey or cream fleece for bib
Iron-on interlining for ears
Pink fleece for insides of ears
Approx. 3 m ($3^1/_4$ yd) white dress net for tail and pom-poms

SPATS

Fleece scraps from costume, or similar colour of felt
Black elastic, 2 cm ($^3/_4$ in.) wide, for stirrups

GENERAL EQUIPMENT

Pins
Fabric scissors
Tape measure
Pinking shears
All-purpose latex adhesive
Hot or cold melt glue gun and glue sticks (optional)
Strong thread
Leather needle
Thimble
Fine-tipped marker pen
Contact adhesive
All-purpose clear adhesive
Chopstick
Materials for dyeing (optional)
Foam or pin board
Wire cutters
Paper scissors
Long glass-headed pins or T-pins, for attaching decoration to hat

Bunny suit

1 Cut out the bunny suit front, back and sleeves from dark grey or brown fleece, and from lining fabric. Tack the fleece pieces onto the corresponding lining pieces.

2 With right sides together, machine stitch the two back pieces together, leaving an opening in the centre back for the zip as marked on the pattern. With right sides together, machine stitch the two front pieces together along the centre front. Insert the zip into the centre back seam (see page 12).

3 With right sides together, machine stitch the back to the front along the shoulder, side and inside leg seams.

4 With right sides together, aligning the edges of the darts, pin and machine stitch the darts at the tops of the sleeves. With right sides together, pin and machine stitch the underarm seams.

5 Turn the sleeves right side out. With right sides together, aligning the underarm seams with side seams on the bunny suit, pin and machine stitch the sleeves to the suit. Notch the curved shoulder seams and press the seams open.

6 Cut out the casings for the ankles and wrists from cotton fabric. With right sides together, machine stitch the casings to the bunny suit at the ankles and wrists. Fold the casings over to the inside of the suit. Pin and slipstitch the casings to the lining, leaving the ends open. Using a safety pin, feed the elastic through the channels, sew the ends of the elastic together and slipstitch the casings closed.

7 Cut the neck binding from the pale grey or cream fleece. Bind the neckline (see page 18).

8 Cut out the bib from pale grey or cream fleece. Pin, then slipstitch it in place on the front of the bunny suit.

Useful Tip

If the strips of net for the tail do not look gathered enough, simply gather again on top of the existing gathering.

Ears

1 Cut out four ears from dark grey or brown fleece and two ears from iron-on interlining. Iron the interlining to the wrong side of two of the fleece ears. Note that the interlining stops short of the seam allowance; it should not get caught in the seam.

2 Cut two inner ear pieces from pink fleece. Machine or hand stitch the inner ear pieces onto the fur side of the other two ear pieces. You do not need to turn under the edges of the fleece – just brush the fur over the join to soften the edge.

3 With right sides together, machine stitch one interlined piece to each of the remaining ears, leaving the bottom edge open. Notch the curved seams and turn right side out.

4 Catch both sides of the bottom of the ear together (marked A to A on the pattern), and stab stitch (see page 11) in place on the bonnet. This gives the ear curve. Trim any uneven layers at the bottom; no need to hem.

Tail

1 Using pinking shears, cut two strips of white net 13 cm (5 in.) wide across the width of the fabric. With the stitch length set to short-to-medium, ruche the fabric down the centre of each strip by pushing the fabric tightly together, using both hands, as it goes under the foot of the machine (see page 14). Run a second row of stitching on top of the first for strength.

2 Fold along the ruched line and topstitch over this line. Hand stitch the strips of net together into a spiral. If you need to join on another strip, just overlap it by about 1 cm (½ in.).

3 Hand stitch the tail onto the backside of the bunny suit, just below the zip.

Pom-poms

1 Using pinking shears, cut five 10 x 150-cm (4 x 60-in.) strips of dress net.

2 Ruche the strips and stitch into tight spirals, as in Step 2 of the tail.

3 Hand stitch three of the pom-poms onto the centre front of the bib of the bunny suit as indicated on the pattern. Reserve the other two pom-poms for the fronts of the spats.

Spats

1 Cut the spat 'uppers' from fleece or felt.

2 Machine stitch the pieces together (see page 20) and attach elastic stirrups to the sides of the spats, checking the correct length first on the child.

3 Stitch a pom-pom to the front of each spat.

Speedy Shortcut

Instead of making spats , buy ready-made fluffy slippers in a colour that matches the bunny suit.

Easter bonnet

You will need

EASTER BONNET

Simple straw hat
Scraps of green felt or reinforcing fabric
Hair comb
Length of elastic, 8 or 10 mm (³/₈ –¹/₂ in.) wide, preferably
    flesh coloured, for chin strap
Approx. 2 m (2 yd) light green organza, organdie or net, for
    hat band, edging and 'lettuce' frills
Length of blue moiré or taffeta fabric for hat ribbon
4 x 5 mm x 36 mm cable ties to strengthen ears (optional)

CARROTS

Polyester wadding off-cuts or small sheet foam 1 cm (¹/₂ in.)
    deep
25 cm (10 in.) orange stretch velvet or Lycra
Pieces of 'lettuce' organza from hat materials

RADISHES

10 cm (4 in.) red or pink stretch velvet or Lycra
Small polystyrene balls 2.5–3 cm (1–1¹/₂ in.) in diameter
10 cm (4 in.) white stretch velvet or Lycra
Red or pink fabric dye (optional)
Pieces of 'lettuce' organza from bonnet materials

FLOWERS AND GREENERY

1 packet light blue tissue paper
1 packet lilac tissue paper
1 packet orange tissue paper
1 packet yellow blue tissue paper
1 packet yellow green tissue paper (option for greenery
    around flowers only)
Pieces of cane, straws or (spent) long matches for stems
1 m (1 yd) green organza, organdie or net for foliage

1 If you can only find an adult-sized hat, follow the
directions for re-sizing the tricorne hat for the Pirate
(page 127). Cut three small pieces of felt or other
reinforcing fabric, using pinking shears if the fabric is
frayable, and glue them in place on the inside of the
bonnet, using all-purpose latex adhesive.

2 Draw around the patches on the inside of the
bonnet, at the points where you are going to attach
the comb and the ears. Apply hot or cold melt glue and
bond the patches firmly to the straw to reinforce the
bonnet at these points.

3 Using strong thread, sew the hair comb to the centre
front of the hat on the inside, with the teeth of the
comb facing inwards.

4 Stitch an elastic strap slightly forward of the halfway
mark on the hat, to be worn either under the chin or
around the back of the head.

Edging and hat band (optional)

1 Using pinking shears, cut a strip of light green
organza, organdie or net fabric on the bias 4 cm
(1¹/₂ in.) wide. Bind the outside edge of the brim (see
page 18).

2 Cut a 58 x 6-cm (23 x 2¹/₂-in.) strip of green organza
for the hat band. Fold it in half, machine stitch along
the long edge to form a tube, then turn right side out.
Pin the band around the base of the crown and fix with
hot or cool melt glue or stitch it in place.

Lettuce frills

1 Using pinking shears, cut 12 lengths of lettuce fabric 5 cm (2 in.) wide and as long as possible on the bias. (If you are using dress net, the strips can be cut straight.)

2 Using a short straight stitch, pleat along one long edge of the strips. The tucks do not have to be exactly the same size, but it is important that they are quite deep so that there is plenty of fullness in the frills.

3 Machine stitch close zigzag stitching over the first line.

4 Pin, then stab stitch the frills in rows around the underside of the brim. Use big stitches, and make sure that the stitches do not cut through the straw.

5 Pin, then hand stitch the blue moire hat ribbon under the brim so that the bonnet can be tied on.

Attaching the ears

1 Pin the ears to either side of the crown where it meets the brim. If the ears flop over, stiffen them by inserting one or two wide cable ties, tapered end first – one at the front and one at the back. Trim the protruding ends of the cable ties to take off any sharp corners, and glue the ends in place with a glue gun.

2 Stab stitch through both thicknesses of the ear, the straw and the felt patches on the inside of the hat.

Useful Tip

When you're stitching through several layers, as you are when attaching the ears, use a leather needle, pulling it through with pliers if necessary, and wear a thimble to protect your sewing finger.

Carrots

1 Using a fine-tipped marker pen, mark out carrot patterns on foam and cut out. Apply contact adhesive (see page 8) along both edges of the 'cone' shape, leave until touch dry, and glue together edge to edge. Apply glue to the edge of the top circle and to the inside of the top of the carrot cone and leave until touch dry. Insert the top circle into the top of the carrot and press together.

2 Cut out the carrot covers from orange stretch velvet or Lycra. With right sides together, pin, tack and then machine, using a stretch stitch. Trim the seam at the pointed end. Turn right side out.

3 Slide the cover over the foam carrot shape. Gather the fabric in tightly by hand at the top, leaving a small hole in the centre for the stalk.

4 Take a small piece of lettuce frillage about 4 cm (1¹/₂ in.) long, fold it in half and then fold it again, then stab stitch through it several times at the base to form a 'stalk' about 1.5 cm (³/₄ in.) long. With the needle and thread still attached, wrap the thread tightly around the stalk to bind it and finish with a few stitches to secure it.

5 Glue one end of the stalk to the foam inside the centre of the gathered carrot cover, then secure with a few stitches to ensure that the carrot top is upright.

Radishes

1 Cut out the radishes from red or pink stretch velvet or Lycra. Run a line of gathering stitch by hand around the dotted line on the pattern, and pull the fabric around the polystyrene ball as tightly as possible. Stitch securely, and cut off any excess fabric above where you have sewn.

2 Cut out the roots from white stretch velvet or Lycra. With right sides together, pin, tack and machine with a stretch stitch. Turn right side out and poke the pointed end with the chopstick to get a sharp point.

3 The dyeing step is not essential, but it adds a lovely subtle touch. Make up the fabric dye, following the manufacturer's instructions. Wet the fabric, then dip the wide (open) end of the root in the dye, at the top. (Wetting the fabric first prevents a hard dye line.) Rinse, squeeze out excess water, then either pin to a piece of foam board or lay on a piece of kitchen towel to dry. If the dye bleeds a little, that's fine; it adds to the organic vegetable look!

4 When the roots are dry, pin them around the sewn end of the radish, stretching them slightly around any 'stump' that is there. Slipstitch around the root to secure.

5 Finally, add a little greenery at the other end, exactly as for the carrot tops but a little smaller.

Showerproof flowers

For longer lasting (showerproof) flowers, use fabric or net instead of tissue paper. Follow the instructions for making the organza lettuce, but gather the fabric more tightly, and hand stitch it into rounds to make rosettes. (This is basically the same technique as for making pom-poms.) Fill the small gap in the middle by sewing on a circle of a contrasting fabric. Spray with fabric protector spray.

Speedy Shortcut

Another – and slightly quicker – way of making the carrots is to make the carrot covers and stuff them tightly with wadding, pushing the wadding in with the chopstick. It doesn't matter if they look a bit lumpy and bumpy: carrots usually are!

Flowers and greenery

1 For the flowers, cut strips 4 cm (1½ in.) wide across the width of the tissue-paper roll. Cut through as many layers of the roll as possible at once, using non-fabric scissors. For the greenery, cut strips 8 cm (about 3 in.) wide for the basket greenery and 4 cm (1½ in.) wide for the flower greenery (as per patterns) in the same way.

2 Cut scallops (or spikes for the greenery) along one edge through as many as 16 thicknesses at once depending on your scissors. Mark out the scallops from the pattern, or cut them by eye if you prefer.

3 Take individual strips of tissue paper, and run a thin line of clear adhesive close to one edge, halfway along the strip. Carefully pin the strips, glue side up, to the top of a foam or pin board and allow to dry for five minutes or so. Glue four or five strips at a time; if you prepare too many, the glue may dry completely before you have time to complete the flowers.

4 When the glue has dried to a tacky consistency, roll up the strips, ruching as you go (it's like rolling a cigarette). With both hands, make tiny little tucks, squeezing the glued edge together with one hand and pulling the un-glued edge out with the other. Pin up to dry.

5 For the stems, take pieces of cane, straws or long matchsticks. Cut to 7 cm (3 in.) long for the big flowers, 5 cm (2 in.) for the small ones. Run a little more clear glue along the gathered edge of the tissue paper strip, then pin it back on the board until it is tacky, as before. Wrap the gathered strip around the stem about two-thirds of the way down, making sure that you are not spiralling down the stem as that will create a pointed flower. For small flowers, use one strip, and for big flowers, use two strips of gathered tissue paper.

6 Cut the stem with wire cutters and spiral a narrow strip of green organza or tissue-paper greenery around the stem.

Adding greenery to flowers

1 Either use strips of the gathered lettuce fabric that was used for the brim, carrot and radish tops, or make up some smaller greenery out of green tissue paper. Using a hot or cold melt glue gun or clear glue, apply adhesive around the base of the strip of foliage and wrap it around the base of the flower.

Decorating the Easter bonnet

1 Arrange the flowers, carrots and radishes on the bonnet to check the layout. It's a good idea to take a digital photo that you can refer back to as you attach the pieces one by one.

2 Attach the flowers and vegetables using a hot or cool melt glue gun or contact adhesive. Alternatively, using big stitches that are not too tight, sew each piece in place.

Useful Tips

Do not use your fabric scissors to cut the tissue paper, as they will quickly blunt.

It is helpful to look at things in a mirror during the making process, as it gives you a different perspective and the ability to see things more objectively. I often leave things overnight and look at them afresh in the morning to see if it looks good at first glance. You quickly notice the weak points in this way.

Space Man

This is a great project for any budding model makers or DIY dads, grandads and uncles to help with (preferably ones with a tool kit!). The control dials are made from empty food containers such as yoghurt pots and coloured plastic tops from drinks bottles. Your young space cadet will have great fun helping to choose what to use, so this costume is something that every member of the family can be involved in making.

You will need

SPACE SUIT

White cotton drill
White cotton quilted lining fabric, preferably with cotton on both sides
Zip to fit
Large hook-and-eye fastening
Approx. 3 m (3¼ yd) cotton webbing tape, 3.5 cm (1⅜ in.) wide
Approx. 80 cm (32 in.) white loop Velcro, 2.5 cm (1 in.) wide

HELMET

White 6-mm (¼-in.) Fun Foam
Clear vacuum-formed plastic packaging for visor
Other half of Velcro used on suit
20 cm (8 in.) white gaffer tape
2 x small white self-adhesive Velcro tabs to hold visor open
Assorted flip-top bottle lids in red, white or blue

BACKPACK AND CONTROL PANEL

Cardboard box approx. 12 x 33 x 48 cm (4¾ x 13 x 19 in.) for backpack
Cardboard box approx. 10 x 20 x 29 cm (4 x 8 x 11½ in.) for front control panel
4 x plastic milk or juice cartons with screw-on tops slightly larger than the diameter of the tubing
Scraps of 6-mm (¼-in.) Fun Foam
Matt white spray paint
Approx. 2 m (2 yd) white cotton or nylon webbing, 4 cm (1½ in.) wide
30 cm (12 in.) white Velcro
2 m (2 yd) convoluted plastic tubing, 3 cm (1¼ in.) in diameter for 'oxygen pipes'
Items of your choice to decorate the boxes – for example, clear or white plastic food trays from supermarkets, coloured plastic bottle tops for control knobs, yogurt cartons, corrugated cardboard, metallic scouring pads

SPACE BOOTS

White cotton drill
Pair of cheap Wellington boots
White elastic, 2.5 cm (1 in.) wide, for stirrups

GENERAL EQUIPMENT

Pins
Fabric scissors
Tape measure
Craft knife and cutting mat
Contact adhesive
Hot or cool melt glue gun and glue sticks
White gaffer tape

Space suit

1 Cut out the pieces for the front, back and sleeves from cotton drill. Cut out two of each piece from quilted lining fabric. Tack each cotton drill piece to two layers of quilted lining fabric.

Useful Tip

Two layers of lining give the necessary bulk, but if you're worried that the suit will be too hot, use only one layer.

2 With right sides together, machine stitch the two back pieces together, and insert the zip in the centre back (see page 12). With right sides together, machine stitch the two front pieces together along the centre front.

3 With right sides together, machine stitch the front and back together along the side and inside leg seams. Turn the body suit right side out.

4 With right sides together, aligning the edges of the darts, pin and then machine stitch the darts at the tops of the sleeves (see page 14). With right sides together, pin and machine stitch the underarm seams. Repeat to make the second sleeve.

5 Turn the sleeves right side out. With right sides together, aligning the underarm seams with the side seams of the body suit, pin and machine stitch the sleeves to the suit. Notch the seams.

6 Cut two collar pieces from cotton drill and one from quilted lining fabric. Tack the lining fabric to the back of the collar. Assemble the collar (see page 16) and attach it to the neckline of the body suit.

7 Hand stitch a large hook-and-eye fastening to the back of the collar.

8 Turn under and pin the cuffs and hems, and slipstitch around.

9 Cut four 3.5 x 9-cm (1⅝ x 3½-in.) strips of cotton webbing. Hand stitch a tab of hook Velcro to each one. Machine or hand stitch the strips of webbing around the outside of the collar, as marked on the pattern. (These will attach to tabs of loop Velcro on the underside of the helmet.)

Useful Tip

Check the straps for length before sewing. If the child has a very long neck, for instance, the straps may need to be longer. There should be no slack, or the helmet will wobble.

Helmet

1 Cut out the helmet top, base, sides, back, front and centre-back strengthener from Fun Foam.

2 Using a craft knife on a cutting mat, cut two ventilation holes and an opening for the visor in the front panel. (If the plastic food container that you are using for the visor is not exactly the same shape as the pattern, trace the outline of your container onto the front panel, making sure that you position it centrally.)

3 Cut the two side edges of the front of the helmet at an angle of 45°. Glue the centre-back seam edge to edge, using contact adhesive (see page 8). Reinforce the centre-back seam with the strengthener, also glued with contact adhesive. Glue the angled side edges to the edges of the front and back panels to complete the 'walls' of the helmet.

4 Cut a hole in the base, following the pattern, so that the helmet will fit over the child's head. Glue the tabs of loop Velcro to the underside of the base, aligning them with the webbing-and-Velcro straps on the collar. Glue the base panel and top of the helmet within the walls of the helmet, so that they are flush with the edge.

5 Take a length of white gaffer tape the same length as the top edge of the visor. Lay a second piece of gaffer tape lengthways down the centre of the sticky side of the first piece of tape and fold it back on itself over the piece it is stuck to. Stick the adhesive side of the gaffer tape to the top of the visor and glue the non-adhesive side to the front panel of the helmet. Make sure that it is not so tight that the visor will not open.

6 To keep the visor open, stick a small tab of Velcro (no bigger than 2 cm/³/₄ in. square) on each side of the outside of the top of the visor and to the corresponding points on the front of the helmet where they touch down.

7 Glue discs of Fun Foam inside the bottle lids to create a flat gluing surface, then glue the bottle lids to the side walls.

Backpack and control panel

1 Collect the decorations and the boxes for the backpack and front control panel together. Plan where everything will go and spray anything that needs to be painted with white paint.

2 Mark out in pencil the position of the different elements on the cardboard boxes, leaving space for the webbing straps that will go over the shoulders and around the sides of the body. Cut webbing straps to the correct length and add Velcro fastenings. Glue the webbing to the front and back boxes, about 4 cm (1¹/₂ in.) in from the top and side edges.

3 Cut the milk or juice cartons to the required depth for the oxygen tubes and mark on the boxes where the tubing will feed through. Trace around the cut-down cartons on Fun Foam and cut the foam shape slightly smaller, so that it fits snugly inside. Cut holes in the stoppers the same diameter as the tubing.

4 Glue the stoppers into the containers using contact adhesive or hot or cool melt glue (if hot, cool slightly, so it will not melt the plastic). Cut holes in the tops of the screw-on bottle tops big enough to feed the tubing through. Now cut the holes in the sides of the backpack box where the tubing goes inside; it should be a tight fit. Push the tubing into one hole on the

Useful Tip

A hot glue gun is generally the best way to attach the components. However, hot glue melts some plastics so, for the larger containers, cut a 'stopper' out of Fun Foam and glue it in place to give you a better gluing surface. For flat items such as corrugated cardboard, double-sided carpet tape works well.

backpack box, thread it through and bring it out on the other side until both ends of tubing protrude by about 75 cm (30 in.).

5 Thread the tubing through two of the containers and screw tops and glue them in place on the sides of the backpack. Glue the other two containers to the sides of the front control panel. (Do not connect the other ends of the tubing to the front control panel until the boxes have been decorated.)

6 Decorate the boxes with the rest of the components, being sure to include a few coloured lids for 'control knobs' so that the space suit isn't completely white. Seal the boxes and tape closed with white gaffer tape.

Space boot covers

1 Cut out the boot cover sides and centre pieces from white cotton drill. Check the size of the paper pattern against the boots before you cut the pieces out. Machine stitch the seams. Clip the curved seams, open up and topstitch on either side using a zigzag stitch.

2 Machine or hand stitch one side of the elastic stirrup under the sole of the boot covers.

3 To cover the boots, pull the boot cover over the top of the boot. You may need to pinch the boot top to get the ankle part of the cover through, as this will be narrower. It should be a tight fit without buckling the boot. Hand stitch the other side of the elastic stirrup in place.

Space gloves

Buy a second-hand pair of white padded ski gloves or mitts.

Speedy Shortcut

Instead of making the boot covers, buy a second-hand pair of white snow or ski boots.

Mervin the Martian

Inspired by the 'little green men' of 1940s and '50s sci-fi movies, this funky-coloured Martian looks all set for a bit of inter-galactic mischief! Green foam nodules, spiky fingers and antennae add a suitably alien touch and contrast well with the green of the body suit; red and green are complementary colours which always look dramatic together.

You will need

BODY, BALACLAVA AND COWL

Lurid green two-way stretch Lycra (for balaclava and cowl, if needed)
Green Velcro (for back of balaclava and cowl, if needed)
All-over nylon Lycra unitard in either white or lurid green
Approx. 30 cm (12 in.) green Velcro, 2.5 cm (1 in.) wide, to attach head to balaclava

NODULES

Approx. 10 x 1.5 m (60-in.) lengths of 2.5-cm (1-in.) foam cord
Green fabric dye
Table salt

HEAD, ANTENNAE AND FINGERS

2 or more (strong, if available) balloons, medium size
Plastic food wrap
1-2 packets green tissue paper, or newspaper
Green and white acrylic or spray paint (if using newspaper)
Hook Velcro to correspond with that already sewn to the balaclava
Green nodules to decorate head
1 length of foam cord
Red fabric dye
2 foam or ping-pong balls about 6 cm (2½ in.) in diameter
1 ping-pong ball for the pupils
Large sheet bright red Funky Foam

SPATS

Green felt
Black elastic, 2 cm (¾ in.) wide, for stirrups
Nodules to decorate
Black pumps or lightweight shoes

GENERAL EQUIPMENT

Pins
Fabric scissors
Tape measure
Old saucepan and wooden spoons or laundry tongs, for dyeing
Rubber gloves and apron, for dyeing
4 or more trouser hangers with clips
Double-sided adhesive tape, 2.5 cm (1 in.) wide
Large piece of stiff cardboard
Mask and disposable plastic gloves
Contact adhesive
Marker pen or tailor's chalk
Polythene sheeting or plastic bags
PVA glue
Talcum powder
Balloon pump (optional)
Masking tape
Heavy bowl or saucepan
Craft knife or scalpel
Black marker pen or acrylic paint
Stapler and staples

Costume base

The base of this costume is a ready-made Lycra unitard. At a small extra charge, some manufacturers will custom make unitards to the colour and measurements that you want and can incorporate a balaclava. You may be able to buy a second-hand unitard, but you will probably have to make and dye your own balaclava. The easiest option is to buy a full cat suit with balaclava, although you may have to have it made especially. Alternatively, opt for a high-necked unitard with a zip up the back and make your own balaclava, or buy a unitard with a scooped neck and back, which would require you to make your own balaclava and cowl.

Balaclava and cowl (if required)

1 Cut out the balaclava sides, centre panels, and cowl from green Lycra. (You will need an inner and an outer layer.) Assemble the inner and outer balaclavas separately (see page 21), leaving an opening in both centre backs for the Velcro.

2 Place the inner and outer balaclavas right sides together, machine stitch around the face opening and turn right side out. Topstitch around the face opening by hand or machine to keep

Useful Tip

Round off the Velcro corners to stop them from scratching.

the two layers together. Tack the open edges together around the outside and centre back edges, then zigzag both layers together on the tacked edges.

3 Assemble the cowl (see step 5, page 21). Machine stitch the balaclava onto the cowl around the neck.

4 Machine or hand stitch loop Velcro pieces onto the balaclava, as indicated on the pattern. Insert the Velcro in the centre back seam.

Dyeing the nodules

1 The foam cord used to make the nodules comes in a cream colour, but it can be dyed. Mix the dye with salt in an old saucepan, following the manufacturer's instructions. Test-dye a small piece of foam first, to get a better idea of the final colour; it will dry lighter.

Useful Tip

The dye is extremely hot, so take great care when removing dripping items from the dye pot or allow it to cool before you remove it.

2 Coil each length of foam cord so that it fits into the saucepan and immerse it in the dye. With the dye on simmer, the foam will quickly absorb the dye; the length of time you leave it depends on how intense you want the colour to be. Don't worry if the dye appears patchy; it all adds to the effect and there is no reason why the nodules should all be the same.

3 When you have the depth of colour that you want, remove the foam coils from the dye with wooden laundry tongs or an old wooden spoon, and rinse out any excess dye.

4 Clip the ends of the foam to trouser hangers. Hang them from the shower head or outside on a washing line and allow to dry thoroughly.

Making the nodules

1 Cut the dry cords to the desired lengths. The nodules can all be the same length, or they can be longer in the middle of the body and shorter on the arms and legs, as on our costume. The shortest ones are about 4 cm (1½ in.) long and the longest 6 cm (2½ in.). The nodules can either be left with simple cut ends or, if you have time, rounded.

2 To round the ends, apply several rows of 2.5-cm (1-in.)-wide double-sided tape to a large piece of stiff cardboard and peel off the protective backing. Cover one cut end of each nodule with contact adhesive (see page 8). Place the un-glued end of each piece on one of the strips of the double-sided tape until touch dry.

3 Continue gluing the ends of nodules for 10 to 15 minutes. Remove the nodule that you glued first from the strip of tape. Carefully pinch the sides of each glued end together to form a rounded end.

Useful Tips

When glueing on the nodules, it is better that the suit is slightly overstretched than understretched, as any glued areas will no longer stretch. Bear this in mind when gluing anything onto a Lycra garment. Do not glue too many nodules onto it and leave plenty of gaps so that the fabric will still be able to stretch. Do not try to sew the foam nodules on, as the foam will only tear and fall off.

4 Continue in this way, alternating between gluing the ends and pinching them together once the glue has touch dried.

Applying nodules to unitard

1 Dress the child in the unitard. Using a marker pen, mark out dots where the nodules should go. You can either do this randomly or attach them neatly in rows. If you opt for the neat row option, stagger each row.

2 Take the unitard off the child. Stuff the unitard with polythene sheeting and bags, or even inflated beach balls, until it looks as if someone is wearing it. If you have any used cardboard tubes, cover them in plastic food wrap and insert them into the arms and legs of the unitard. Alternatively, trace around your child on flat cardboard, cut out and cover the cardboard with plastic food wrap.

3 Apply glue to the cut end of each nodule. While the glue is still wet, stamp the glued end on one of the marked dots on the padded-out suit. As the suit has polythene or cling film behind it, if the glue soaks through the fabric, the fabric should still peel off the polythene fairly easily when you un-stuff it.

4 Continue until the entire suit has been covered in nodules. Once the glue has dried thoroughly, remove the stuffing from the unitard. If it has stuck in places, give it a good tug to pull it away. The polythene will tear before the Lycra does, so you can pull it quite hard. Dust the inside of the suit with talcum powder to stop any glue on the inside sticking to itself, and hang somewhere airy, preferably outside or in a well ventilated area, until the smell of glue has worn off.

Head

1 Insert one balloon inside the other for a stronger base, but a single balloon is also fine. Pour some water into the balloon to help stabilise it while you are working on it, and blow it up to the size that looks right for the dome of the Martian's head. Check the balloon against the size of your child's head to make sure the proportions look right.

2 Take a heavy bowl, the right size to sit the base of the balloon into. Cover the bowl with plastic food wrap to protect it from the PVA glue mix. Position the blown-up partially water-filled balloon in the bowl and lightly tape the edge to the bowl to stabilise it. (It might become top-heavy when it is covered with the wet newspaper.) Make sure that the area that needs to be covered to create the dome is outside the rim of the bowl.

3 In a disposable container, mix PVA glue and water to the consistency of single cream. Tear tissue paper or newspaper into pieces about 10 cm (4 in.) long and, wearing disposable plastic gloves, dip them into the paste. (Newspaper is strong, but will need to be painted afterwards; I used tissue paper the colour that I wanted.) Lay the paper over the balloon and smooth it down carefully. Repeat, overlapping each piece a little, to cover the entire surface of the balloon and allow to dry.

4 Repeat until you have built up at least six layers of paper. Make sure you cover all areas as evenly as possible to avoid creating any weak areas that might collapse later.

5 Remove the papier maché piece from the base, pop the balloon and peel it out. Treat the dome gently – it is not very strong. If it accidentally tears, patch it on the inside with masking tape. If it seems too thin and weak, paint a little undiluted PVA glue over it to strengthen it more, or apply more strips of masking or gaffer tape on the inside. If you have used newspaper rather than coloured tissue paper, paint the dome to match the unitard.

6 Check that the dome fits around the top of the child's head. If it is too small or too tight, cut a little off at a slight angle to increase the circumference. If it is too big, as mine was, cut a straight line down the centre back of the dome, and overlap as much as you need, fastening the edges together with Velcro. This creates a little 'extra-terrestrial' point at the top of the head, which looks great.

7 Now try the domed head on the child again, and mark with a fine marker pen, on the

Lycra balaclava as well as on the dome, where it meets the head and how much of an overlap there is, if any. Cut away the dome around the ears to create a helmet shape.

8 On the inside of the dome, glue pieces of hook Velcro at the base of the overlap, across the forehead and at each temple, making sure that the Velcro pieces line up exactly with the Velcro tabs on the balaclava.

9 Glue nodules of green foam cord onto the dome.

Antennae

1 Following the instructions for dyeing the nodules, dye one length of foam cord red to make the antennae.

2 Dye two foam balls red for the eyes, to match the antennae, or paint foam or ping-pong balls red.

3 Using a craft knife or scalpel, carefully cut a ping-pong ball in half to make the two pupils. Using a marker pen or acrylic paint, paint the pupils black.

4 If the curve of the ping-pong ball is smaller than that of the red eyeball, cut a disc of foam from the cord and glue it to the flat side of the ping-pong ball pupil. Then glue the pupils to the red eyeballs. Glue the eyeballs to the ends of the antennae, making sure both eyes are looking in the same direction. (Or you might prefer to make your Martian cross-eyed!)

5 Glue the other ends of the antennae to the right angle to glue to the forehead of the papier maché head and butt glue together.

6 Store the head on an upturned vase or a kitchen-roll holder so that the antennae are leaning backwards rather than forwards, as they will 'reform' to the position they are kept in.

spiky fingers

1 Cut ten 42 x 2-cm (16½ x ¾-in.) strips of red Funky Foam. Cut the corner off one end, as shown on the pattern. This is the end that you start rolling.

2 Place a strip of 1-cm (½-in.) double-sided tape along one long edge of the foam and peel off the backing paper. Start rolling evenly and tightly at an angle of about 45°. When you reach the end, staple to secure, and flatten the staples with pliers to prevent them from scratching the child.

3 The claws are worn jammed straight onto the ends of the child's fingers, and secured with a little double-sided tape – but make some spares in case they fall off and get lost. Alternatively, glue the claws onto gloves, as for the Fiery Dragon (page 111).

Spats

1 Cut the spat 'uppers' from a matching colour of felt.

2 Machine stitch the pieces together (see page 20) and attach elastic stirrups to the sides, checking the correct length first on the child. With the shoes inside the spats to form a solid base on which to glue, decorate the spats with nodules in the same way as for the body.

Heavenly Angel

Attired in a shimmering white robe studded with star-shaped sequins, this angel will steal the show at any school nativity play. The 'feathered' wings are attached to a separate harness and are designed to fold back for easy storage and transportation. They are quite time-consuming to make, but you could get your little angel to help by drawing around the individual feather shapes.

You will need

DRESS

White crepe dress fabric
Zip to fit
Small hook-and-eye fastening
Approx. 30 cm (12 in.) white loop Velcro, 2.5 cm (1 in.) wide, for back of bodice
Approx. 2 m (2 yd) white bias binding, 1.5 cm (³⁄₄ in.) wide, for wrist casings
White elastic, 1 cm (¹⁄₂ in.) wide, for wrist elastics
Star sequins
Clear or silver seed beads
Beading needle and thread

WINGS AND HARNESS

84 x 60-cm (36 x 24-in.) sheet of 5-mm (¹⁄₄-in.) foam board
1 small roll packing foam
32 x 5-mm x 36-cm white cable ties
Approx. 30 cm (12 in.) white hook Velcro, 2.5 cm (1 in.) wide, for inside of harness

Approx. 15 cm (6 in.) white loop Velcro, 2.5 cm (1 in.) wide, for back of strengthener
Approx. 1.5 m (60 in.) white cotton webbing, 3.5 cm (1³⁄₈ in.) wide, for shoulder straps
Approx. 1.5 m (60 in.) white string to tie back wings

HALO

60 cm (24 in.) narrow stranded nylon boning
5mm x 36-cm cable tie
Approx. 1 m (1 yd) 6.4-mm clear heat-shrink tubing
43-cm (17-in.) length of 4-mm dowel
Approx. 15 cm (6 in.) white hook Velcro, 2.5 cm (1 in.) wide
100 g (4 oz) silver or holographic sequin centres glitter

GENERAL EQUIPMENT

Pins, safety pins
Tape measure
Pinking shears
Fine-tipped marker pen
Craft knife and cutting mat
PVA adhesive (optional, for repairs)
Duct or gaffer tape
Corkscrew for making holes in wing frame
Double-sided adhesive tape, 2.5 cm (1 in.) wide
Double-sided carpet tape
Wire cutters
Hot air gun or powerful hairdryer
All-purpose clear adhesive

Dress

1 Using pinking shears, cut out the skirt back and front from white crepe. With right sides together, machine stitch the back and the front together, leaving a gap in the centre back for the zip, and press the seams flat.

2 Gather the top of the skirt (see page 13), so that the skirt circumference measures the same as the bottom edge of the bodice.

3 Using pinking shears, cut out two bodice fronts, four bodice back panels and the collar pieces from white crepe. With right sides together, machine stitch the shoulder and side seams of the bodice panels, leaving the centre backs open for the zip. Gather one long edge of the collar to fit around the neckline. With right sides together, sandwiching the collar in between, join both layers together by pinning and sewing around the neckline. Clip the curved seam, turn right side out. Press.

4 Tack around both layers of the armholes, the centre back and along the bodice hem, so that the fabric cannot slide around.

5 With right sides together, pin and machine stitch the gathered skirt to the bodice.

6 Insert the zip in the centre back (see page 12). Sew a small hook-and-eye above the zip.

7 Hand stitch the loop side of a 13 x 2.5-cm (5 x 1-in.) strip of white Velcro on either side of the zip, as indicated on the pattern, on the right side of the bodice. (The other half of the Velcro will be attached to the inside of the wing harness to keep it steady.)

8 Using pinking shears, cut out the sleeves from white crepe. With right sides together, machine stitch along the underarm seams and press the seams flat. Pin white bias binding 1.5 cm (³/₄ in.) wide around the inside of the sleeves, as marked on the pattern. Turn under the ends of the bias binding and topstitch along both edges to form a casing for the wrist elastic.

9 Gather the sleeve head (see page 15), as indicated on the pattern, so that it fits the armhole.

10 Using a safety pin, feed elastic through the wrist casings. Hand stitch the ends of the elastic together.

Speedy Shortcut

If time is tight, you could carefully glue the sequins in position.

11 With right sides together, aligning the underarm seams with the side seams and the centre of the sleeve head with the shoulder seam, pin and machine stitch the sleeves into the armholes. Clip the curved seams.

12 Stitch silver star sequins all over the dress, adding a clear or silver seed bead in the centre of each star.

Wings and harness

1 Pin the wing frame pattern to foam board and draw around it with a fine-tipped marker pen. Remove and repeat as a mirror image to make the second wing. Cut out, using a craft knife on a cutting mat.

2 Cut out the double slots for the webbing straps at the top of the back plate and the single slots at the side, as marked on the pattern. Take care not to cut too far, or too close to the edge or the foam may break. (If it does break, repair it with PVA glue and gaffer or duct tape.) Using a craft knife, chamfer (angle) the top edge along the front of the wing frames.

3 Cut out the one-piece strengthener for the back plate (the second layer) in the same way. Cut double slots in the strengthener, too.

4 Score, but do not cut right through, the front of the wings as marked on the pattern, then strengthen the score line by covering it with a strip of duct or gaffer tape. This will enable the wings to fold back.

5 Using a corkscrew, make holes in the wing frames, as marked on the pattern. Strings will be threaded through these holes later, to make it easier to store and transport the wings.

Feathers

1 Mark out feathers on the roll of packing foam by drawing around the templates with a fine-tipped marker pen. The length of the feathers should run down the length of the roll of packing foam.

2 Cut out the feathers, cutting inside the marked line to get rid of the ink lines. Cut notches in the feathers, either by eye or by tracing around the notches in the pattern. You will need a right and a left wing, so remember to cut the feathers in mirror images. The box below sets out how many of each size to cut.

3 For the feathers in Row 1, cut narrow strips of double-sided tape across the width of the tape, approx.

NUMBER AND SIZE OF FEATHERS REQUIRED FOR EACH ROW

ROW 1: Flight feathers with cable tie quills (applied to back of wing frame)

Size 1: 6 right, 6 left	Size 2: 2 right, 2 left
Size 3: 4 right, 4 left	Size 4: 4 right, 4 left

ROW 2: Feathers without quills (applied to front of wing frame)

	Size 5: 7 right, 7 left
Size 6: 7 right, 7 left	Size 7: 6 right, 6 left

ROW 3: Feathers without quills (applied to front of wing frame)

	Size 7: 6 right, 6 left
Size 8: 8 right, 8 left	Size 9: 5 right, 5 left

ROW 4: Feathers without quills (applied to front of wing frame)

	Size 9: 5 right, 5 left
Size 10: 12 right, 12 left	Size 9: 7 right, 7 left

5 mm (¼ in.) wide. Remove one side of the backing paper and press the strips onto the cable ties, starting at the tapered end of the cable tie. Remove the other side of the backing paper and, starting 4–5 cm (1½–2 in.) from the tips of the feathers, apply the cable tie to the packing-foam feathers, pressing firmly.

4 Apply strips of double-sided carpet tape to the back of the wing frame as close together as possible.

5 Starting with the largest 'flight' feathers (those with quills), in Row 1, peel the paper away from the double-sided tape on the back of the wing frame and press each cable tie 'quill' in position. Using wire cutters, cut off any cable ties that protrude beyond the frame.

6 Work from the outside of the wing towards the centre, overlapping feathers as you go. If your work space is large enough to lay out both wings, do one row on one wing and then the same row on the opposite wing to ensure that they are symmetrical.

7 To cover up the exposed cable tie ends at the back of the wing, cut a layer of packing foam in the shape of the wing frame, ending where the back plate strengthener starts, and stick it on with double-sided tape.

8 Turn the wings over and repeat the process with the double-sided tape on the front of the frame, then apply Rows 2, 3 and 4. The double-sided tape on the bone area will be covered by the time you get to the smaller feathers. When this happens, apply more double-sided tape on top of the feathers already in place. Alternatively, on the quill-less feathers, place a small tab of double-sided tape on each feather and apply the feathers to the wings.

Useful Tips

If your scissors get gummed up, spray them with spray machine lubricant or WD40.

Keep checking your layout against the pattern as you work: the feathers should radiate out from the 'elbow' bend of the wing like a fan, so do not lay them next to each other in parallel lines.

Print the pattern out on tracing paper, so you can see both sides easily and overlay it on the wings.

Joining the wings and Forming the back plate

1 Join the two halves of the wings together at the centre back, using a strip of strong duct or gaffer tape on each side. This will form the back plate. (The strengthener does not need to be joined at the centre back.)

2 Using double-sided carpet tape, apply two strips of hook Velcro on either side of the centre back line the length of the inside of the back plate. These correspond with the strips of loop Velcro on either side of the dress zip and will stop the wings from wobbling.

Back-plate strengthener

1 Aligning the double slots, fix the strengthener to the back plate at the back of the wings, using strips of double-sided carpet tape. Keep the tape to the inside of the back plate and away from the slots and edges.

2 Along the centre back of the strengthener, stick a 15-cm (6-in.) strip of loop Velcro 1 cm (½ in.) wide. The corresponding strip of hook Velcro on the halo upright will affix to this.

Shoulder straps

1 Cut two lengths of webbing for shoulder straps long enough to go all around the shoulder, under the arm, and fold back, like the straps on a backpack. Slot each length of webbing through one of the double slots in the back plate and stab stitch (see page 11) through to secure.

2 With the child wearing the dress, it's now time to have a fitting. Another pair of hands would be very useful at this point. Fix the Velcro on the back of the dress to the Velcro on the front of the back plate. Take the shoulder straps over each shoulder and around under the arms. Slot the end of the webbing through the slot in the strengthened back plate and back on itself. Mark with safety pins where you need to sew a tab of Velcro onto the ends of the webbing to make the straps adjustable, so that the wings can be worn by another child.

3 Finally, thread through the strings that will hold back the wings (unles you prefer the wings to be opened out at their full span). Tie a knot big enough not to slip through hole (A) on the wing, thread the other end of the string through from the front to the back, then across to the hole (A) at the top of the back plate.

Treatment and Storage of Wings

The wings are delicate, so treat them carefully! If any feathers fall off or slide to one side, simply reposition them and press back, or apply a little more double-sided tape.

Although the foam is very thin, it is quite resilient. To transport the wings, tie both wings together at the end of the wing frame by threading fine string through holes (B) and tying together in a bow.

Store the wings, either flat or folded, somewhere out of the way such as the top of a wardrobe. Opened out flat, hanging on a wall hook from the tapes, they will make quite a nice wall hanging!

Central heating may cause the double-sided tape to dry out and the feathers to drop, but they can be re-applied.

Halo

1 Make a hoop of nylon boning 16 cm (6¼ in.) in diameter and zigzag stitch the ends to secure.

2 Attach a cable tie around the join, positioning it at right angles to the halo. Slide the heat-shrink tubing along the cable tie. Slide the dowel into the heat-shrink tubing. Using a heat gun, direct hot air onto the tubing to shrink it and grip the cable tie and dowel firmly together.

3 Stick a 15-cm (6-in.) strip of hook Velcro along the length of the upright, to correspond to the strip of loop Velcro on the centre back of the back-plate strengthener.

4 Bit by bit, apply clear adhesive to sections of both sides of the boning and, while the glue is still wet, sprinkle liberally with glitter. The halo may initially sag under the weight, but it should firm and lighten up once the glue has fully dried.

5 Attach the halo to the back plate at the last minute, before the party or play begins.

Useful Tip

If heat-shrink tubing is not available, bind the cable tie with electrical tape or masking tape.

heavenly angel 67

wily wizard

Cosmic powers are clearly at work here, as a veritable galaxy of stars, moons and ringed planets adorns this shimmering, midnight-blue wizard's robe and pointy hat. And of course, no self-respecting spell-master would be without a wand to conjure up tasty treats and make his enemies disappear in a puff of smoke. Simple to stitch, this costume is pure magic!

You will need

ROBE

Satin velvet for the robe
Approx. 4 m (4¼ yd) fusible bonding web
Iron-on interlining for collar
Approx. 30 cm (12 in.) each of gold, purple, red and green lamé or other metallic fabric for appliqué
2 gold tassels for ends of ties
Small black hook-and-eye fastening for neck
2 beads approx. 6 mm in diameter

HAT

1 long grey or white wig (optional)
Black, blue or white Fun Foam or Funky Foam
Fabric from robe to cover hat
Metallic fabrics as used on robe appliqué
1 cat's bell
Length of 1-cm (½-in.) elastic for chinstrap, if needed

SHOES

2 of the appliqué fabrics (or felt for the spats and an appliqué fabric for the toes)
Fusible bonding web (optional)
Black elastic, 2.5 cm (1 in.) wide, for stirrups
Packing foam, Funky Foam or 1-cm (½-in.) foam rubber for base cone of pointed toes
2 cat's bells
Wadding to stuff pointed toes

MAGIC WAND

Scraps of metallic fabrics from costume
92-cm (36-in.) length of balsawood rod, approx. 1 cm (½ in.) in diameter
Double-sided adhesive tape

HAREM PANTS

Indian metallic gauze
Approx. 1 m (1 yd) elastic, 2 cm (¾ in.) wide, for waist and ankles
Approx. 1 m (1 yd) elastic, 2 cm (¾ in.) wide, for braces (optional)

GENERAL EQUIPMENT

Pins, safety pins
Tape measure
Fabric scissors
Fine-tipped marker pen
Non-stick silicone baking paper
Hot or cool melt glue gun and glue sticks
Pinking shears

Fabrics

Before you buy your fabric, consider how different fabrics behave. It is also important to think about the hat covering at the outset: it is useful to have some stretch in the hat fabric, whereas too much stretch in the robe will make it sag.

Satin has a mind of its own, especially when cut on the bias, so it is tricky to seam smoothly. It also tends to fray a lot, sometimes even after it has been pinked.

Any kind of velvet slides around and should be tacked together before it is machined. The big advantage of a stretch velvet is that it does not fray. For a very opulent robe that will really upstage, go for a shot silk taffeta or dupion, which has highlights of a second colour – deep blue with red, for example. The important thing is to find a nice rich colour and surface, which these fabrics will give. Just make sure you don't choose anything that's too girly!

Robe

1 Cut out the robe front, back, sleeves and collar from your chosen fabric.

2 Following the manufacturer's instructions, apply fusible bonding web to the back of each appliqué fabric. Using the templates provided, draw around as many of the motifs as you can fit in on the paper backing of the bonding web. (Test your marker pen first, as the backing paper is resistant to some pens, while other pens just smudge.)

3 Cut out the motifs and remove the backing paper. Protect the ironing board with non-stick silicone baking paper and place the motifs, one by one, web side down, on the garment pieces. Place another sheet of baking paper on top, then press with a hot iron to fuse the motifs to the robe fabric. Avoid placing motifs on the seams; half a planet does not look as good as a whole one!

4 Machine stitch the centre front and centre back seams of the front and back panels, stopping where indicated on the centre front pattern to form a slit at the neck.

5 With right sides together, machine stitch the side seams and the shoulder seams of the front and back panels together. Press the seams open.

6 With right sides together, pin and machine stitch the sleeve underarm seams. Press the seams open.

7 Turn the sleeves right side out. With right sides together, aligning the underarm seams with the side seams and the centre of the sleeve head with the shoulder seam of the robe, pin and machine stitch the sleeves into the armholes.

8 Cut out the front and back collar pieces and the interlining. Following the manufacturer's instructions, iron the interlining to the back of one collar piece, just inside the seam line. Assemble the collar (see page 16) and attach it to the neckline of the robe.

9 Apply strips of fusible bonding web to the hems and cut with pinking shears. If you opt for pinked edges, cut out the pattern pieces using pinking shears.

Tassels and tie cords

1 For the tassel ties, cut two 80 x 4-cm (32 x 1½-in.) strips of metallic fabric in different colours. Fold each one in half, right sides together, and machine stitch along the long raw edge to form two thin tubes.

2 Attach a safety pin to one end of each tube, then feed the safety pin through the tube and out the other end, pulling the fabric through until it is all the right way around. Repeat with the second tube to make two long cords.

3 Attach a tassel to one end of each cord.

4 Stitch one cord to each side of the collar to form the tie fastening. Sew a hook-and-eye fastening in addition to this if you wish. Cover the sewn ends of the cords with beads.

Hat

1 Measure the circumference of the child's head, adding a little bit extra to allow for a seam allowance and for the hem of the hat covering to be turned under at the base.

2 Cut the cone-shaped base from Fun Foam (6 mm/¼ in.) or Funky Foam (2 mm). If you are using the thicker Fun Foam, do

not include a seam allowance; glue the long sides of the cone together edge to edge, or baseball stitch (see page 11) together. If you are using thin Funky Foam, overlap the seam allowance and glue, or pin and stab stitch along the overlap; you may need to zigzag stitch two sheets of Funky Foam together to get a large enough piece.

3 Cut out the fabric covering and decorate it with appliqué planets, avoiding the seams. The pattern for the covering is bigger than that for the base to allow for the outside curve and the seam allowance. A bit of stretch in the fabric will make it easier to obtain a smooth fit. If you are using a stretch velvet, machine stitch the seam using a shallow zigzag or stretch stitch. If you are using a non-stretch satin, one or both of the centre back seams will be on the bias, which could make for a wobbly-looking seam, so pin, tack and hand stitch carefully. Turn the hem under at the base and either stab stitch through the covering and base foam or glue in place.

4 Roll in the excess fabric at the very top of the cover and slipstitch it into a narrow roll to form a sharp point.

5 Run a line of running stitch from the tip of the foam cone right up to the end of the excess fabric. Gently pull the thread to gather the fabric into a curve. Once the gathers are even and the curve is at the angle you want, secure with a few hand stitches.

6 Sew a cat's bell onto the end of the curved section. If the cat's bell is so heavy that it drags the point of the hat down, feed a strand or two of filament from nylon boning into the hat to give it some spring.

7 Sew an elastic chinstrap to either side of the hat, slightly behind each ear, if needed.

Shoes

1 Cut the spat 'uppers' from two colours of the planet fabrics. If the fabric you are using for the planets is very fine, back it onto a stronger backing such as felt using fusible bonding web. Alternatively, use felt for the spats and the metallic fabric for the pointed toes only.

2 Machine stitch the pieces together (see page 20) and attach elastic stirrups to the sides, checking the correct length first on the child.

3 Now make the pointed toes. (This process is like making up miniature versions of the hat.) Cut the base cones from Funky Foam. Make up the cones in the same way as the hat, with the seam running along the front of the toe, and cover with fabric. Stuff with wadding. Hand gather the seam into a little spiral curl, as at the very top of the hat, and hand stitch a bell sewn to the end of each toe.

4 Hand stitch the pointed toes to the toes of the spats, adjusting the angle as necessary. Do this with the shoes inside the spats to make a firm base and to get the placing right. Alternatively, pin the base of the pointed toes to the toes of the spats, mark the position and glue in place with hot or cool melt glue.

Magic wand

1 Glue a small square of metallic fabric to each (circular) end of the rod. Trim the fabric flush with the edge when dry.

2 Cut strips of metallic fabric 3 cm (1¼ in.) wide. You will need the longest strips you can cut, as you will spiral them up the rod to cover it. Place a strip of double-sided tape around either end of the rod, and cover with one strip. This will avoid gaps at the ends of the rod as the spiralled strips will not cover the entire end. Run a strip of double-sided tape down the length of rod. Spiral the fabric strip around the rod at an angle. Take care to keep some tension in the fabric to avoid getting little folds and wrinkles.

3 Now cut strips of fabric in a contrasting colour, 1.5 cm (³/₄ in.) wide. Put tabs of double-sided tape at the ends of the rod and repeat the spiralling process, leaving gaps between first and second colours, so that you end up with something that looks like a barbershop pole or a candy cane. As long as the fabric is fixed at both ends, you do not need to apply tape all the way along the rod, although an occasional tab of double-sided tape here and there is a good idea.

Harem pants

1 Cut out the front and back pieces from metallic gauze.

2 With right sides together, machine stitch the inside leg seams. With right sides together, machine stitch the crotch seams together.

3 Turn under along the fold line at the top of the waist and topstitch to form a channel 3 cm (1¼ in.) deep, leaving an opening at one side seam through which to thread the elastic.

4 Attach a safety pin to one end of a length of 2-cm-(³/₄-in.)-wide elastic and feed the elastic through the channel. Hand stitch the ends of the elastic together.

5 Turn up the hems and pin and topstitch to form a narrow casing. Attach a length of narrow elastic to a bodkin or safety pin, thread the elastic through the casing and hand stitch the ends of the elastic together.

6 Turn the pants right side out. If necessary, machine stitch elastic braces at the front of the pants, cross them over at the back and machine or hand stitch at the back after checking the length on the child.

Rag Doll

A traditional rag-doll costume, with gingham frock, patch pockets and simple white apron, is a really cute look for a little girl's party. Note that, apart from the collar, this costume has raw, intentionally frayed hems – a simple touch, which has the additional benefit of cutting down on sewing time for busy mums!

You will need

DRESS, APRON AND BLOOMERS

Large-checked pink gingham for dress
White dress net for petticoat
Small-checked blue, red and brown ginghams for patches
Approx. 1 m (1 yd) fusible bonding web
Red, white and blue embroidery silks
Fine white cotton (lawn or fine turban), for apron and lining
White zip to fit
1 small silver hook-and-eye fastening

Iron-on interlining
Approx. 1.5 m (60 in.) white bias binding, 1 cm (½ in.) wide, for knee and wrist casings
Approx. 1.5 m (60 in.) white elastic, 1 cm (½ in.) wide, for knees and wrists
2 x white buttons, 2.5 cm (1 in.) in diameter
Approx. 2 m (2¼ yd) elastic, 2 cm (¾ in.) wide, for bloomers, braces and waist
Two pairs spotted or striped tights, different colours

1 pair black or red Chinese slippers
2 small back buttons (if none on Chinese slippers)

GENERAL EQUIPMENT

Pins, safety pins
Tape measure
Fabric scissors
Non-stick silicone baking paper

Dress

1 Cut out the skirt from the large-checked gingham and the petticoat from net. Pin and machine stitch the skirt and petticoat side seams together separately, leaving an opening at the top of the centre back seam for the zip. Press the seams open. Note that the net hangs down below the skirt.

2 Cut out the skirt patches from the small-checked ginghams, as marked on the pattern. Following the manufacturer's instructions, apply fusible bonding web to the back of each patch, leaving the edges of the patches free of the bonding web so that they can fray. Protect the ironing board with non-stick silicone baking paper (not greaseproof paper), and place the patches web side down on the skirt. Place another sheet of baking paper on top, then press with the iron to fuse the patches to the dress fabric. Topstitch the patches by hand, using embroidery thread, taking care not to gather the edges.

3 Gather the top of the skirt and the petticoat (see page 13), so that the skirt circumference measures the same as the bottom edge of the bodice. Secure the ends of the gathering threads with knots.

4 Cut out the bodice front and back pieces from the dress fabric and from the white cotton lining fabric. With right sides together, machine stitch the shoulder and side seams of the inner and outer bodice pieces together, leaving the centre back open for the zip.

5 Machine stitch the outer bodice to the skirt and petticoat.

6 Insert the zip in the centre back of the outer bodice (see page 12). Sew a hook-and-eye fastening above the zip.

7 Cut out two left and two right collar pieces from large-checked gingham and two pieces from iron-on interlining. Following the manufacturer's instructions, iron the interlining to the back of one left and one right collar piece, just inside the seam line. Assemble the collar (see page 16). Trim the curved seams, turn right side out and press carefully.

8 With right sides together, pin the inner and outer bodices together, sandwiching the collar in between and making sure that both halves of the collar align with the centre front of the neckline. Machine stitch the layers together around the neckline and clip the curved seam.

9 Machine stitch around the armholes of the outer and inner bodices to hold the layers together.

10 Cut out the sleeves from large-checked gingham and the sleeve patches from small-checked gingham, as indicated on the pattern. Using fusible bonding web, apply patches to both sleeves, leaving the edges free of bonding web so that they can fray. Topstitch the patches, using embroidery thread, as for the skirt patches.

11 Gather the sleeve heads (see page 15), as indicated on the pattern, so that they fit the armholes.

12 With right sides together, machine stitch the underarm seams and press. With right sides together, aligning the underarm seams with the side seams of the bodice and the centre of the sleeve head with the shoulder seam, pin and machine stitch the sleeves into the armholes. Clip the curved seams.

13 On the inside of the sleeves, machine topstitch bias binding 6 cm (2½ in.) up from the edge of the cuff, as indicated on the pattern, turning under the ends. This forms a casing for the wrist elastics.

14 Using a safety pin, feed 1-cm-(½-in.)-wide elastic through the casings. Hand stitch the ends of the elastic together.

Apron

1 Cut out the apron pieces from white cotton. The skirt has a double layer and raw frayed edges. Topstitch around the edges of the skirt 1.5 cm (³⁄₄ in.) from the edge, making sure that both layers are perfectly flat.

2 Machine stitch two parallel rows of gathering stitching 1 cm ($\frac{1}{2}$ in.) apart around the top edge of the skirt, as indicated on the pattern (see page 13), then pull the threads to gather the skirt to fit the apron bib.

3 Cut out the double pocket from white cotton and topstitch it onto the right-hand side of the apron skirt, stitching through all layers.

4 Cut out the waistband, shoulder straps and ties on the fold. Following the manufacturer's instructions, iron interlining onto all pieces.

5 Fold the waistband in half along the fold, right sides together, and machine stitch, leaving the centre of the bottom edge of the waistband open as marked on the pattern. Turn right side out and press flat.

6 Machine stitch the apron skirt onto the centre of the waistband, turn the seam allowance up into the waistband, and slipstitch the other side of the waistband down, covering the seam allowance.

7 With right sides together, fold the shoulder straps in half along the fold and machine stitch along the long raw edge and one short edge. Turn right side out and press. Turn under the seam allowance at the open end and slipstitch closed.

8 Hand stitch the shoulder straps over the waistband, as indicated on the pattern. Using red and blue embroidery thread, sew one button to the top of each strap. Check the length of the shoulder straps on the child, turn under the seam allowance at the open end of the shoulder straps and slipstitch closed. The other end of the shoulder straps can then be sewn to the back of the waistband, crossing over at the back.

Bloomers

1 Cut out the bloomer pieces from white cotton. With right sides together, machine stitch the inside leg seams. Press the seams flat.

2 Turn over the seam allowance at the waist and machine stitch to form a channel 3 cm (1¼ in.) deep.

3 On the inside of the knees, pin and machine topstitch a strip of bias binding, as indicated on the pattern, to form casings for the knee elastics. Feed narrow elastic through the casings. Hand stitch the ends together.

4 Feed 2-cm- (¾-in.) elastic through the waist channel. Hand stitch the ends together. Turn the bloomers right side out.

5 Machine stitch the elastic braces at the front of the bloomers, cross them over at the back and machine or hand stitch at the back.

Hair

Tie strips of gingham in bows all over the child's head. If she has short hair, pin bows into the hair with hair grips.

Tights and shoes

1 Use two contrasting pairs of striped or spotted tights. Cut one leg off each pair of tights just below the crotch. Join the leg that you have cut off to the other pair of tights at the crotch, using a zigzag stitch.

2 Find Chinese slippers with a cross strap and attach two buttons.

Mini-me rag doll

You will need

25 cm (10 in.) medium-weight calico for doll's body
20 cm (8 in.) polyester wadding, or polystyrene beads or
  kapok
1 chopstick
50 cm (20 in.) small-checked pink gingham for dress
30 cm (12 in.) plain fine white cotton (or scraps from dress)
  for apron and bloomers
20 cm (8 in.) each of tiny-checked red, blue, brown and pink
  gingham (or scraps from dress) for patches
20 cm (8 in.) fusible bonding web
Approx. 1 m (1 yd) white cotton tape, 2.5 cm (1 in.) wide, for
  apron straps and ties
2 x 1-cm (½-in.) buttons for eyes
2 x 1-cm (½-in.) buttons for apron
Red embroidery thread (or red cotton thread for mouth)
Red and blue thread
Curved needle
Strong off-white, cream or beige thread

Doll's body

1 Cut out the pieces for the doll's body, head, arms and legs from calico. With right sides together, machine stitch around the body and head, leaving the necks of both pieces open to allow for stuffing. Machine stitch the arms and legs in the same way, leaving the ends that join onto the body open. Notch the seams and turn all the pieces right side out.

2 Stuff each piece tightly with wadding, polystyrene beads or kapok, pushing each piece in with a chopstick or the end of a pencil before adding the next piece. If you want a floppy doll, it is the joints that make it floppy, so do not stuff right to the ends. For a solid doll that will not flop over, stuff full, leaving only the seam allowance un-stuffed so that you can turn it in afterwards.

3 Turn in the seam allowance on the arms and legs and pin the pieces to the body. Hand stitch around all the joints.

Dress, apron and bloomers

1 Cut the pieces for the dress from pink gingham and the pieces for the bloomers and apron out of the plain white cotton.

2 Machine stitch double rows of gathering stitches, as indicated on the pattern, along the top edge of the apron, the waist of the bloomers, and both knees on the bloomers.

3 With right sides together, machine stitch the side and inside leg seams of the bloomers. Turn right side out. Gather the knees and waist to the required length and secure the threads by knotting. Gather the top of the apron to the required length and secure the threads.

4 Cut out patches in different colours of gingham and apply them to the dress. (You can either apply them using fusible bonding web and then topstitch with decorative stitching in one or two strands of embroidery silk, or stitch them straight on.)

5 Machine stitch double rows of gathering stitch, as indicated on the pattern, all around the top edge of dress skirt and on both sleeve heads and wrists. With right sides together, machine stitch the centre back seam of the skirt and the underarm seams of sleeves. Pull the gathering threads to gather the fabric to the required length. Secure the gathering threads by knotting them.

6 Assemble the bodice and bind the neck edge of the bodice with a bias strip cut from gingham.

7 Fray all the hem edges to a depth of about 2–3mm (1/8 in.).

8 With right sides together, machine stitch the skirt to the bodice. Put the dress on the doll, threading the arms carefully through the armholes. Pin both sleeves over the arms, onto the bodice, turning in the seam allowance and matching the inside seam of the bodice to the seam of the sleeves. Slipstitch by hand.

9 Turn under the seam allowance along the gathered edge of the apron and hand stitch it to the front of the skirt, where it meets the bodice.

10 Make up the straps and waistband of the apron using 2.5-cm (1-in.) white cotton tape folded in half.

Sew the buttons on to the front with a single strand of red and blue embroidery silk.

11 Make up a false bow and two long ties using the 2.5-cm (1-in.) white cotton tape (not folded). Hand stitch the ends of the ties to the centre back of the apron waistband. Sew the bow on top of that. Cut the ends of each tie diagonally.

12 Put the bloomers on the doll and stitch them to the doll's body around the waist.

Head and hair

1 Sew on the button eyes. Lay a piece of red embroidery silk in a curve on the face to make a big smile and carefully pin it in place. Stitch around the 'smile' with a needle and red thread. If you find this too fiddly, just stitch the mouth in back stitch, using red embroidery thread.

2 Tear strips of the fine white cotton about 1 cm (1/2 in.) wide. Sew three strands together at the top and plait into 8-cm (3-in.) lengths, securing with a few stitches at the base.

3 For the hair ribbons, cut or tear strips of tiny gingham in a mix of all the colours you have. Fray the edges slightly.

4 Pin the plaits onto the back of the head and around the seam, pointing upwards, and hand stitch them in place. When they fall back down over the stitching, they will stick out slightly from the head. Now tie hair ribbons to the base, middle and end of each plait, securing with a stitch to stop the ribbons from sliding off.

5 Using a small, curved needle and strong calico-coloured thread, hand stitch the head to the body at the neck.

Useful Tip

If you want a particular colour of hair, buy coloured cotton or dye the strips to get the colour you want.

Gypsy Dancer

A swirly patchwork skirt in three brightly coloured layers forms the basis of this design – ever so simple to stitch if you need to create a costume in a hurry. I've included instructions on how to make the blouse, too, but you could buy a ready-made one.

You will need

SKIRT AND BLOUSE

Three contrasting patterned fabrics for skirt
Approx. 70 cm (27½ in.) elastic, 2.5 cm (1 in.) wide, for waistband
Approx. 1 m (1 yd) elastic, 2.5 cm (1 in.) wide, for braces
Fine cotton lawn or poplin, preferably off-white, for blouse
Bias binding, 1 or 1.5 cm (½ or ¾ in.) wide
Approx. 2 m (2¼ yd) white elastic, 6 mm (¼-in.) wide, for blouse waist, cuffs and neckline

FOR THE COIN BRACELET

30–40 assorted small coins
Small jump rings
Ready-made chain bracelet

FOR THE COIN NECKLACE

Approx. 30 red beads in different sizes and shapes
Approx. 30 long, ready-made headpins
Small jump rings

Chain necklace with links about 8 mm (⅛ in.)
30–40 assorted small coins

ANKLE BRACELET

Approx. 25 cm (10 in.) red or black elastic, 1.5-cm (¾-in.) wide
12–15 gold or silver cat's bells

GENERAL SEWING EQUIPMENT

Pins, safety pins
Tape measure
Pinking shears (optional)

GENERAL JEWELLERY-MAKING EQUIPMENT

Cola to clean coins
Piece of wood to drill into
Protective glasses
Drill and 1.5 mm (¹⁄₁₆-in.) drill bits
Needle file
Fine-nosed pliers
Wire cutters

ROSE

Pink and red tissue paper
Paper scissors
All-purpose clear adhesive
3-cm (1¼-in.) piece of cane or (spent) long matchstick

Fabrics

Find three different cotton prints for the skirt, preferably lightweight such as lawn. The fabrics should not be stiff, as the skirt needs to move. Alternatively, make the skirt out of remnants to make a patchwork; just seam the fabrics together to make up the required lengths, making sure that you keep the grain straight and consistent.

Skirt

1 Referring to the patterns, cut or tear the skirt fabrics into strips of the right widths. Machine stitch them together if necessary to make up the correct lengths. Machine stitch the short ends of the strips together to form three large circles.

2 Fold over the top edge of the top layer by 5 mm (1/4 in.). Then fold over the top edge again by 4 cm (1½ in.) and machine topstitch to form a casing, leaving an opening at the seam through which to thread the elastic.

3 Gather the top edge of the middle and bottom layers of the skirt (see page 13), so that each layer measures the same as the bottom edge of the previous layer. Secure the ends of the gathering threads with knots.

4 With right sides together, machine stitch each layer onto the bottom of the previous layer.

5 Using a safety pin, thread the waistband elastic through the waistband channel. Hand stitch the ends of the elastic together.

6 If braces are required, hand stitch elastic braces to the back of the skirt. Fit the skirt on the child, cross the braces over at the back, and hand stitch them to the front of the waist.

7 Leave the hem as a raw edge; you can either fray it or cut it with pinking shears.

Blouse

1 Cut out the front, back and sleeves from cotton lawn or poplin. With right sides together, machine stitch the back to the front along the shoulder and side seams and turn right side out.

2 Turn under the neckline and hem, as marked on the pattern, and topstitch. (Alternatively, leave pinked or frayed for speed.)

3 Pin and machine stitch 1.5-cm (3/4-in.) bias binding around the waist, as marked on the pattern, as a casing for the elastic. (You can use ready-made bias binding, or cut strips on the bias from the blouse fabric.)

4 With right sides together, machine stitch the sleeve underarm seams. Turn right side out.

5 With right sides together, aligning the underarm seams with the side seams of the bodice, pin and machine stitch the sleeves into the armholes. Clip the curved seams.

6 Pin and machine stitch 1.5-cm (3/4-in.) bias binding around the wrists and neckline, as marked on the pattern, turning under the ends.

7 Using a safety pin, thread 6-mm (1/4-in.) elastic through all the casings. Hand stitch the ends of the elastic together.

Coin bracelet and necklace

1 Place the coins in a container filled with Cola overnight or until they are clean and shiny. Wash and dry the coins.

2 Place a coin on the block of wood. Wearing protective glasses, drill a hole about 2 mm (1/16 in.) away from the edge of the coin. Repeat this on all coins.

3 Using a needle file, file away any burrs in the metal until all the coins are smooth.

4 To make the bracelet, using fine-nosed pliers, open up a jump ring, loop it through the hole in the coin

> **Useful Tip**
>
> Do not make the waist elastic too tight or it will ride up and stay up; it should be loose enough to drop back down when the gypsy dancer lowers her arms.

and through a link in the bracelet chain, then close the jump ring again. Repeat until all the coins have been attached to the chain.

5 To make the necklace, thread the red beads onto ready-made headpins. Using wire cutters, cut the headpins, leaving about 1 cm (½in.) wire extending below the bead. Using fine-nosed pliers, bend the extending wire into a loop just below the bead, and wrap the excess wire around the wire stem. Open up a jump ring, hook it through each loop and through a link in the necklace chain, then close the jump ring again.

6 Repeat step 4 to complete the necklace, alternating coins and red beads.

Ankle bracelet

1 Cut a length of coloured elastic long enough to fit around the child's ankle.

2 Sew cat's bells around the elastic at 1-cm (½-in.) intervals. Measure the elastic around the child's ankle and hand stitch the ends of the elastic together. Make sure there is no thread linking each bell to the next or it will stop the elastic from stretching, which is necessary as there is no fastening.

Rose for hair

1 Make up a paper rose for the hair, following the instructions for the flowers for the Easter Bunny's hat on page 46.

Shawl and scarf

There are plenty of interesting inexpensive scarves and shawls in markets. A fringed shawl can be folded diagonally and tied around the hips over the skirt. A belly-dancer's scarf with dangly fake coins works well: trashy is good!

Shoes

On a fine day on the lawn, bare feet would be great, especially set off by the bell ankle bracelet; otherwise, opt for a simple pair of pumps or ballet flats.

Snow Queen

Illustrated children's stories and fairytales can be a wonderful source of inspiration for costumes. The idea for this costume originally came from Hans Christian Andersen's story *The Snow Queen*, in which the Queen kidnaps a young boy named Kay and takes him to her palace of snow and ice. The White Witch, in C.S. Lewis's *The Lion, the Witch and the Wardrobe*, is a similarly evil character.

You will need

DRESS

Ice-blue satin crepe
Pale blue zip to fit
500 g (16 oz) iridescent sequin centres
  or glitter
Wadding
Small bag of seed beads in icy colours

PETTICOAT

White acetate or satin lining fabric
Small hook-and-eye fastening
White dress net

CROWN

65 cm (25 in.) white electrical cord,
  6 mm ($\frac{1}{4}$ in.) in diameter
Clear plastic cable ties approx. 19.5 cm
  x 3 mm ($7\frac{3}{4}$ in. x $\frac{1}{8}$ in.)
Clear plastic cable ties approx. 14.5 cm
  x 3 mm ($5\frac{3}{4}$ in. x $1\frac{1}{8}$ in.)
Approx. 2 m ($2\frac{1}{4}$ yd) white dress net to
  make crown edging
Plastic hair comb
40–50 cm (16–20 in.) elastic, 6 mm
  ($\frac{1}{4}$ in.) wide, for chin strap
200 g (8 oz) sequin centre iridescent glitter
Transparent thread (optional)

GENERAL EQUIPMENT

Pins
Tape measure
Fabric scissors
Pinking shears
Beading needle and thread
Micro tagging gun and tags or hot glue
  gun (optional)
Clear spray adhesive
Masking tape

Dress

1 Using pinking shears, cut out the dress front and back panels from ice-blue satin crepe.

2 With right sides together, machine stitch the centre back and centre front seams, leaving an opening in the centre back for the zip. Insert the zip in the centre back (see page 12). Machine stitch the front panels to the back panels along the side and shoulder seams. Clip the curved seams and press open.

3 Again using pinking shears, cut out the top and lower sleeves from blue satin crepe. The lower sleeves are made from a double layer of fabric. Fold each lower sleeve in half, right sides together, and machine stitch the side seams. Press the seams flat and turn right side out. Tack both hem edges of the lower sleeves together.

4 Gather the sleeve heads of the top sleeves (see page 15), as indicated on the pattern. Pull the threads to gather the sleeve heads until they fit the armholes exactly.

5 With right sides together, machine stitch the underarm seams of the top sleeves. Press the seams flat. Machine stitch the top and lower sleeves together, press the seams flat and turn right side out.

6 With right sides together, aligning the underarm seams with the side seams of the dress and the centre point of the sleeve head with the shoulder seam, pin and machine stitch the sleeves into the armholes. Clip the curved seams.

7 Cut out the front and back facings from blue satin crepe and machine stitch together at the shoulder seams. With right sides together, pin and machine stitch the front and back facings around the neckline. Clip the curved seams, then turn the facings to the inside of the dress and press. Catch the facings to the seam allowances of the dress by hand.

8 Decorate the dress with sequin snowflakes, securing them in the centre with a seed bead.

9 Cut the snow shapes for the neckline, cuffs and hem out of wadding. Using a micro tagging gun (see page 19), attach the snow to the dress around the edges and centres of the cuffs and hem. Repeat around the neckline, tagging under the facings wherever possible. Alternatively, work a few small stitches from the back of the piece, in the centre of each snow peak, or use a hot glue gun to attach the snow to the dress – although this is not removable.

Useful Tip

Use as few tags or stitches as possible so as not to pull the fabric of the dress, but make sure that the snow edging is securely attached.

Useful Tips

When using spray adhesive, wear a mask, work in a well ventilated room and protect your work surface with newspaper or a polythene sheet.

Try not to spray glue on the fabric of the dress itself, although a bit of overspill will not matter.

10 Working one small section at a time, spray adhesive onto the wadding snow and then sprinkle on glitter or iridescent sequin centres. Once all the snow has been frosted with the glitter, shake the dress to remove any excess glitter. Sweep up any glitter falls from the protective sheet and re-use it on the crown.

Petticoat (optional for added glamour!)

1 Using pinking shears, cut the petticoat pieces out of lining fabric. Cut away the armhole and neck seam allowances, as these edges are not turned under on the petticoat; the finished edge of the petticoat will be the same as the sewing line of the dress.

2 Machine stitch the centre front and centre back seams, leaving the top of the centre back open, as marked on the pattern.

3 Machine stitch the side seams.

4 Hand stitch a hook-and-eye fastening to the centre back neck.

5 Cut the net into four across the width of the fabric. Ruche along one long edge (see page 14). If the net does not look gathered enough, repeat the process.

6 Using tacking stitches or tags, attach the ruched net

Speedy Shortcut

Glue the sequins on with all-purpose clear adhesive, hot or cool melt glue. Apply glue only to the back on the sequin: if it spreads onto the fabric, it will spoil the look of all your hard work! Do a test piece first to make sure that the glue does not melt the sequin.

strips around the skirt of the petticoat, so that the edge of the net is level with the hem. Use one or two layers of net, depending on how far you want the hem of the dress to stick out.

Crown

1 Form a length of white electrical cable into a circle the right size for the child's head, overlapping the ends by about 5 cm (2 in.). Join the cable into a circle by pulling two short cable ties tightly around the overlap to secure it.

2 Alternating long and short cable ties, tie the cable ties around the cable to form the 'spokes'; they should radiate upwards and outwards. Don't tie them too tightly initially in case you need to slide them along to space them evenly. Once you have gone all the way around, tighten the cable ties to lean outwards; it doesn't matter if the angles vary a little.

3 Cut two 150 x 5.5-cm 60 x 2¼-in.) strips of dress net, one for the inside and one for the outside of the crown. Fold each strip in half several times and pin the layers together. Using the template, cut zigzag shapes along one long edge.

4 Ruche the fabric along the straight edge (see page 14). The gathered strip should be the same length as the circumference of the crown.

5 Hand stitch the ruched edge of the net strips to the base of the crown – one to the inside and one to the outside. Be patient if the thread keeps getting caught around the ends of the cable ties; they do tend to get in the way. You may need to work some extra stitches in invisible thread to tether the net in the middle of the strip and prevent it from fanning out too much.

6 Stitch the plastic hair comb to the centre front of the crown, facing inwards. For added security, add an elastic chin strap.

7 Wrap masking tape around the hair comb (and elastic, if using). Working in small sections at a time, spray glue onto the crown and the net edging, and sprinkle liberally with glitter or iridescent sequin centres. Remove the masking tape from the hair comb when the glitter has been applied.

Shoes

Buy little embroidered Indian slippers. They are usually sparkly, but you can easily add more glitter by sticking on iridescent cup sequins, or sprinkling on the leftover iridescent glitter or sequin centres from the dress.

Warrior

In the Middle Ages, all the fabrics would have been made from fibres such as jute, hessian or flax, so this costume uses mostly natural fabrics. I also 'distressed' and aged the fabrics for an authentic 'battle-stained' look.

You will need

JACKET, TROUSERS, CLOAK AND SHIRT

Hessian or jute sacking for jacket
Black cotton quilting for jacket lining
Scraps of brown leather
4 x 2.5-cm (I-in.) buckles for jacket
Flax or linen for trousers
10 cm (4 in.) black Velcro, 2 cm (³/₄ in) wide, for trouser fastening
Black elastic, 2 cm (³/₄ in) wide, for trouser braces
Flax, jute or linen for cloak
Non-itchy rough cotton for shirt
Bias binding for neck and armholes
White cotton tape, 1 cm (¹/₂ in.) wide, for shirt ties or hook-and-eye fastening

STUDDING

350 metal studs, 1 cm (¹/₂ in.) in diameter
Tourmaline (brown)

CHAIN-MAIL COLLAR (OPTIONAL)

50–60 m (55–65 yd) 3-cm (1¹/₄-in.) nylon cord or string
Brown or black fabric dye
Two pencils or pair of knitting needles
Short, stubby brush
Pewter acrylic paint
Pewter wax or Dutch metal (optional)

GAUNTLETS (OPTIONAL)

20 cm (8 in.) brown felt or leather pieces
20 cm (8 in.) fusible bonding web
1 pair brown, green or grey woollen gloves
10 cm (4 in.) black Velcro, 2 cm (³/₄ in.) wide

BOOT COVERS

Pair of Wellington boots
Brown felt
Black elastic, 2 cm (³/₄ in.) wide, for stirrups
Heavyweight iron-on interlining
Scraps of sponge
All-purpose latex adhesive
Black acrylic paint

BELT

Old leather belt (adult size)
Studs from jacket
Scrap of 5-mm (¹/₄-in.) foam board for belt end
Chocolate wrapper foil
Double-sided adhesive tape or all-purpose clear adhesive
Black matt or brown spray paint or black acrylic paint

GENERAL EQUIPMENT

Pins, tape measure and fabric scissors
Tailor's chalk, or dressmaker's tracing paper and tracing wheel
Leather needles and punch pliers
Plastic sheet or bag
Awl or corkscrew
PVA adhesive
Hot glue gun and glue sticks
Hammer
Strong thread or fine twine
Mid-brown and olive green fabric dye
Basic dyeing equipment for cold dye
Cheese grater, coarse sandpaper, soap or candle wax and gardening gloves
Chopstick
Disposable plastic gloves

Patch dyeing (optional)

Dye fabric before you cut out the pattern pieces – then it doesn't matter if the fabric shrinks during dyeing.

1 Make up the dye following the manufacturer's instructions. Wet the fabric, scrunch it up and put it in the dye pot. Submerge the fabric by about half its bulk.

2 Dye the fabric a patchy brown, then repeat in a patchy green. Dry the fabric and iron it only enough to make it workable; a crumpled texture adds to the character.

Jacket

1 Cut out the jacket fronts, back and sleeves from both hessian and quilted lining fabric. (If you are going to quilt the jacket, buy approx. 10% extra fabric.) Note that the lining is cut shorter than the hessian on the hem edges of the front and back to allow for the fringed hem.

2 Using tailor's chalk or a dressmaker's tracing paper and wheel, mark out the quilting lines on the hessian pieces. Tack all the hessian pieces to the corresponding quilted pieces. Machine quilt the pieces.

3 With right sides together, machine stitch the fronts to the back along the shoulder and side seams.

4 Asemble the collar (see page 16) and stitch it to the neckline of the jacket.

5 With right sides together, pin and machine stitch the sleeve underarm seams. Turn sleeves right side out.

6 With right sides together, aligning the underarm seams with the side seams on the jacket, and the centre of the sleeve head with the shoulder seam, pin and machine stitch the sleeves to the jacket. Notch the curved seams. Hem the cuffs if you wish.

7 Pin one edge of the leather binding strips along both centre fronts of the jacket, as marked on the pattern. Fold the other half of the strips over to the inside and, using a leather needle and strong thread or twine, stab stitch (see page 13) by hand.

8 Antique the buckles using Tourmaline (see 'Studding', opposite). Make up buckles and straps from the patterns and, using punch pliers, punch holes in the straps for the buckle prongs. Poke the centre prongs through the holes and fold the straps back on themselves around the buckle bars.

9 Stitch the buckles to the straps, then stitch the straps to the jacket front, with the corresponding straps aligned on the opposite front.

useful Tip

If the Tourmaline doesn't take, spatter the buckles with matt black spray paint.

Trousers

1 Cut out the trouser front and back pieces and the waistband from flax or linen.

2 With right sides together, pin and machine stitch the front and back pieces together along the outside and inside leg seams, then stitch the crotch seam, leaving the centre front open. Turn the trousers right side out. Turn under and press the seam allowances on the top layer of the centre front opening.

3 Sew Velcro fastening onto the fly front, as marked on the pattern. Add elastic braces (optional).

4 Fold the waistband along the centre fold line, right sides together. Pin and machine stitch the waistband ends. Trim the seam allowances and corners and turn right side out. Press.

5 With right sides together, aligning the raw edges, pin and machine stitch the outer edge of the waistband to the waistline of the trousers.

6 Fold the waistband over to enclose the seam you have just made, then pin and slipstitch it in place on the inside.

7 Hem the trousers, if desired, or leave raw.

Cloak

1 Cut out the cloak from flax, jute, hessian or linen.

2 Cut a 250 x 10-cm (100 x 4-in.) length of the cloak fabric for the neck binding and cloak ties. Matching the centre point of the neck binding and the centre point of the cloak neckline, fold and overlap the neck binding over the cloak neckline. Pin and topstitch along the entire length of the neckline and both ties. Leave the edges and both ends raw and allow to fray.

Shirt

1 Cut out the shirt front and back from rough cotton fabric.

2 Cut a slit in the centre back, as marked on the pattern. Face the centre back slit.

3 With right sides together, pin and machine stitch the front to the back along the shoulder and side seams.

4 Bind the neck, back net slit and armholes with ready-made bias binding (see page 18) or a bias-cut strip of the same fabric (see page 17).

5 Add cotton tape or string ties or a hook-and-eye fastening at the centre back to fasten.

6 Fray the fabric and make small holes around the hem.

Studding

1 To antique the studs, tip a little Tourmaline liquid into a clean, empty, non-metallic container (Tourmaline does not melt plastic). Add the studs and swill them around to coat them, or stir with a chopstick. They should tarnish and discolour almost immediately. When coated, empty the studs out onto a strong plastic sheet. Spread out and allow to dry overnight or dry with a hairdryer.

2 Using an awl or a corkscrew, carefully make holes at each cross-point on the quilted jacket. Poke the ends of each stud through the holes, and open out the prongs flat at the back. To make sure the prongs don't scratch the child, glue small patches of leather or fabric over them.

Chain-mail collar

1 Dye the string before you start knitting, as it may shrink. To prevent tangling, coil the string before you put it in the dye pot and do not agitate it. Note that some synthetic yarns will resist the dye.

2 Using pencils, or knitting needles if you have them, cast on enough stitches to knit a length about 27.5 cm (10¾ in.). Decreasing one stitch at each end of each row, knit until the piece is about 12 cm (4¾ in.) deep and roughly fits around half the neckline edge. Cast off. Knit another collar piece in the same way, then join them edge to edge.

3 Place the finished collar on a plastic sheet and, using a short stubby brush, apply pewter metallic acrylic paint. Allow to dry.

Useful Tip

Make sure that the shank of the studs is long enough to go through both the fabric and the quilted lining, and still be able to open out at the back to keep it in place.

If time is tight, leave the studs off the back of the jacket as the cloak and collar will cover most of it.

4 Generously sponge PVA adhesive on top of the collar and leave until the collar is completely dry. Hammer the knitted piece on a hard surface to flatten it. Highlight the metallic effect with touches of pewter wax or Dutch metal.

5 Hand stitch the chain-mail collar to the jacket around the neckline, with the opening at the centre front. Catch it on the outside of the shoulders, centre fronts and back, so that it doesn't flip back.

Gauntlets

1 Cut out the gauntlet cuff from brown felt, leather or leather cloth. If the fabric is floppy, bond it to felt with fusible bonding web.

2 Hand stitch one side of the gauntlet to the cuff of a glove. Add Velcro tabs to the other side of the glove and the outside of the gauntlet, as marked on the pattern, to enable the child to fit his hand through comfortably. Repeat with other glove.

Boot covers

1 Cut out the boot cover sides and centre pieces from brown felt. (Check the size of the paper pattern against the Wellington boots first.) Machine stitch the seams. Clip the curved seams, open up and topstitch on either side of the seam line using a zigzag stitch.

2 Machine or hand stitch one side of the elastic stirrup under the sole of the boot covers.

3 Pull the boot cover over the top of the boot. You may need to pinch the boot top to get the ankle part of the cover through, as this will be narrower. Hand stitch the other side of the elastic stirrup in place.

4 Cut out the cuff pattern from felt and from iron-on interlining. Following the manufacturer's instructions, iron the interlining to the felt cuff, just inside the seam allowance of the felt.

5 Turn the edges of the felt over the interlining edges all the way around, and topstitch a double row of straight or zigzag stitches to finish.

6 Fold the seam allowance of the boot cover over to the outside of the boot, then pin the wrong side of the top of the cuff to the edge of the seam line. It is better to do this when it is on the boot to keep the shape taut. Make sure that the cuff is centred at the front.

7 Whipstitch (see page 10) the top of the boot cover to the cuff by hand along the very top edge, right around the boot top. The ends of the cuff will stick out at the back. They can either be left open or stitched part or all the way down the back.

8 Distress the boot covers by sponging on a mixture of latex adhesive mixed with a little black acrylic paint around the edges of the feet (optional).

Belt

1 Find an old leather belt you can distress, or a new leather or canvas belt. An adult-sized belt is best, as the end needs to be threaded back through the belt.

2 Punch extra holes with punch pliers if needed to make it fit over the jacket, and add studs as desired.

'Distressing' fabric

This process is fantastic fun, especially if you like to get your hands dirty! Unlike patch dyeing, distressing is best done once the garment has been made up. You will need a cheese grater or surform, sandpaper, soap or candle wax.

Wearing gardening gloves to protect your hands, grate the fronts of the jacket and cloak, elbows and hems, knees and seat. Cut small holes and jagged edges around the edges of the cloak, and fray afterwards.

Rub the shoulders, collar and cuffs with soap or candle wax, to make them look greasy. Drag the costume around the garden, set the dog on it, or even drive the car over it! I also dipped the hem of my cloak into dark dye to make it look weathered. If you are not able to dye your fabrics, put them in a hot wash cycle (if you have bought a little extra fabric to allow for shrinkage).

---

3 Make a fake metal end for the belt by cutting a piece of 5-mm (1/4-in.) foam board, and covering it with a piece of foil or chocolate wrapper. Stick the foil to the foam board belt tip with double-sided tape or all-purpose clear adhesive. Spray lightly with matt black or brown spray paint to age it.

4 Using punch pliers, punch small holes in the wide end of the fake-metal belt tip and the belt end. Sew the belt tip and the belt together, using a double length of strong waxed thread or twine.

Wooden staff

Find a reasonably thick, sound branch to use as a staff from the garden or your local woodland. (Make sure that there are no sharp twigs that could cause damage.) If necessary, sand down any rough or sharp ends to blunt them.

Pocahontas

Beading and fringing are traditionally found on Native American costumes and this design incorporates both. The appliqué motifs are bonded on, using fusible bonding web. I used flowers for a pretty, feminine touch, but you could substitute bird or animal motifs, all of which are readily available to trace from copyright-free sources.

You will need

TROUSERS AND TUNIC

Chamois leather skins or artificial suede cloth (minimum fraying preferably)
Approx. 65 cm (25 in.) elastic, 2.5 cm (1 in.) wide, for waistband
Approx. 1 m (1 yd) elastic, 2.5 cm (1 in.) wide, for braces

APPLIQUÉ, BEADED TASSELS AND FRINGING

Approx. 1 m (1 yd) suede cloth or chamois leather skins for fringing and appliqué
Fusible bonding web
Assorted beads
Beading thread

HEADBAND

Strip of suede cloth or chamois leather, 2 cm (¾ in.) wide
2 quills (feathers), cut down from bottom of quill if too tall
Beads as used on costume

MOCCASINS

Suede cloth or chamois leather remnants from costume
Approx. 60 cm (24 in.) bias binding, 1.5 cm (¾ in.) wide, in beige or any of the appliqué colours
Approx. 1 m (1 yd) narrow millinery elastic or cord as drawstring
Sturdy insoles

GENERAL EQUIPMENT

Pins
Tape Measure
Straight fabric scissors
Pinking shears
Coloured marker pens
Non-stick silicone baking paper
All-purpose latex adhesive
Fine-tipped marker pen
Safety pin narrow enough to thread through bias binding
Polythene sheet or bin bag
Talcum powder
Thick beige or brown thread for hand top stitching
Dressmakers' tracing paper and tracing wheel (optional)

APPROX. FRINGING LENGTHS NEEDED:
WIDE: (14cm deep)
Sleeves – 25 cm (10 in.) each sleeve
Tunic hem – 70 cm (27½ in.) front hem, 70 cm (27½ in.) back hem
Tunic sides – 33 cm (13 in.) each side

Trouser sides – 60 cm (24 in.) each side
(Total quantity wide fringing – 3 m 76 cm/13 ft)
NARROW: (5.5 cm/2¼ in.)
Moccasins – 28 cm (11 in.) each moccasin
(Total quantity narrow fringing – 56 cm/22 in.)

Trousers

1 Using pinking shears, cut out the trouser fronts and backs from the chamois leather or suede cloth.

2 With right sides together, machine stitch the outside leg seams. Apply fringing over the outside leg seams on the right side (see opposite), with the uncut part of the fringing strips facing forwards. Then machine stitch the inside leg seams and crotch. Clip the curved seams and turn right side out.

3 Turn the waistband allowance over to the inside at the waist, as indicated on the pattern. Machine topstitch to form a casing 3 cm (1¼ in.) deep, leaving an opening through which to thread the elastic.

4 Attach a safety pin to one end of the elastic for the waistband, and feed a length of 2-cm- (¾-in.)-wide elastic through the channel. Hand stitch the ends of the elastic together, overlapping the ends by about 3 cm (1¼ in.).

5 If necessary, machine stitch elastic braces at the back of the trousers, cross them over at the back and machine or hand stitch at the front after checking the length on the child.

Tunic – appliqué and beading

1 Using pinking shears, cut out the tunic front, back and sleeves from the chamois leather or suede cloth.

2 Following the manufacturer's instructions, apply fusible bonding web to the back of a piece of suede cloth big enough to trace out all the appliqué shapes and fringes. Peel off the paper backing, mark out the flower, leaf, stem and headband shapes on the back of the bonded fabric, and cut out the shapes.

3 Colour in the appliqué shapes using broad-nibbed marker pens and allow to dry.

4 Mark out the placings of the flower and stem shapes on the garment pieces, and also the points where the beaded tassels are to be attached.

5 Protect the ironing board with non-stick silicone baking paper (not greaseproof paper, which can stick), and place the motifs one by one, web side down, on the garment pieces. Place another sheet of baking paper on top, then press with a hot iron to fuse the motifs to the tunic fabric. Start with the centre of the flower, and gradually add all the shapes until all the flowers, petals, leaves and stems have been applied. If stems cross over the seams, do not press them in place until the garment has been completed.

Beaded tassels

1 Mark out strips of suede cloth on the back of the fabric for the two-strand tassels, cutting in the centre, as marked on the pattern, to make two strands joined at the top. You will need about 50 tassels for the front and sleeves of the tunic.

2 Make up strands of beads, working from the bottom up. (Make sure that the beads are securely held by making at large knot at the bottom, or looping the thread through itself around the first bead.) When complete, using the same thread onto which you threaded the beads, sew through the top of the tassel a couple of times and secure the thread at the back.

3 Using a cotton bud, apply dabs of latex adhesive to the tunic and the backs of the tassels, behind the beading stitches. When touch dry, bond the pieces together.

Assembling the tunic

1 With right sides together, machine stitch the front to the back along the shoulder seams. Press open the seams.

2 With right sides together, machine stitch the sleeves to the armholes. Press the seam allowances towards the wrist edges. Topstitch the armhole edges by hand, using visible stitches for a 'hand-made' look.

3 With wrong sides together, machine stitch both underarm seam edges and the side seams. Apply fringing over the seam of each sleeve (see below), with the uncut part of the fringing strips facing forwards.

4 Complete the appliqué stems over the sleeve seams.

To store the lengths of fringing strips before you attach them to the costume, either tape them to a wall or board with masking tape, or pin them to poly-foam board. Do not leave the fringing in a heap or it will crease.

Fringing

1 If your fabric frays, apply fusible bonding web to the back of the fringing fabric following the manufacturer's instructions. Using pinking shears, cut out the fringing strips. Leaving a margin at the top, as shown on the pattern, mark each fringing strand on the back using a fine-tipped pen – or cut them by eye if you feel confident enough. Using straight scissors, cut each strand.

2 Measure out and cut the lengths of fringing that you need for each section of the costume, then pin them to the hem of the tunic, the undersides of the fronts of the sleeves and the side seams (fringing facing backwards) of the tunic and trousers.

3 Protect the fabric with baking sheet paper and, using the tip of the iron, iron along the very top edge of the fringing strips, removing the pins as you go, to fuse them to the garment. For added security, topstitch by hand using a strong thread and stitches about 5 mm (¼ in.) long.

Speedy Shortcut

You do not need to sew the beads on individually: you can continue the thread from one bead to another without cutting, but oversew a couple of times at the back before you 'jump' to the next bead so that they don't slide.

Headband

1 Measure the child's head for the headband. Apply the appliqué shapes to the headband, as indicated on the pattern (see page 96).

2 Check the size of the headband on the child, and join the ends at the back by overlapping. Referring to the pattern, hand stitch two small channels for the feathers, stitching through both layers of the overlap. The feathers should fit tightly and be removable for storage.

3 Sew the beads on by hand, taking care not to 'gather' the headband with stitching that is too tight.

4 Insert the feathers in the channels.

Moccasins

1 Check the child's foot against the moccasin sole and uppers patterns. Cut out the moccasin pieces from suede, suede cloth or chamois. You need a double layer for the soles.

2 Machine stitch the centre front and centre back seams of the uppers, clip the curved seams, open up, and zigzag topstitch down either side of both seams.

3 Machine straight stitch both layers of the double soles together in rows, as marked on the pattern.

4 Fold the ends of bias binding under and machine stitch the bias binding to the right side of the ankle openings, leaving the binding open at the centre back. Turn the binding to the inside and topstitch along the original stitch line, securing on the inside.

5 With right sides together, pin the soles to the uppers, making sure they fit together accurately. Machine stitch, removing the pins as you go. Notch all around the seams between the soles and uppers, taking care not to accidentally cut the seam. Turn right side out.

6 Using a safety pin, thread millinery elastic or cord through the bias binding channel. Remove the safety pin and tie the elastic in a bow. Adjust to fit the child's foot.

7 Turn the moccasins upside down and place on a sheet of polythene. Paint the soles only with three layers of latex adhesive, allowing the adhesive to dry thoroughly between coats. Try not to paint over the seam line onto the upper. Dust with talcum powder to stop the soles sticking to each other.

8 Make fringing as indicated on the pattern, in the same way as for the costume. Hand sew the fringing around the ankle opening to the outside of the bias binding, taking care not to sew through the elastic.

9 Insert a sturdy insole.

Useful Tips

You need to cut one layer of the sole to size and the other one slightly bigger. When you have stitched the two layers together, trim the bigger layer flush to the accurately cut layer. If you try to join two accurately cut layers together, they will move as they are being machined and will not line up correctly.

These moccasins are really slippers and not outdoor shoes. They are best changed into on arrival at the party, especially if it is wet!

Daisy Fairy

This delightful creature has a circlet of daisies around her head, with more daisies on the leotard. Adapt the design by using your own little fairy princess's favourite flowers and colours – perhaps zany, bright pink gerberas with a lime-green leotard for a really funky and exuberant fairy, or bluebells and a silvery leotard for a more delicate look.

You will need

BASQUE AND TUTU

White or ivory dress net
Pink dress net for scalloped edging (optional)
Approx. 1 m (1 yd) pink or white glitter net for petals
Pink sequins or crystals (sew on or hot stones) for petals
Yellow stretch velvet or Spandex for waistband
Yellow Velcro, 2 cm (¾ in.) wide

LEOTARD AND SLEEVES

Yellow stretch velvet or Spandex
White crystal organza for sleeves
White elastic, 5 mm (¼ in.) wide for cuff casings
3 or 4 artificial daisies

WINGS

Extra-stiff net or dress net
Scraps of pink glitter net
Approx. 2 m (2¼ yd) white narrow stranded nylon boning stripped to single strands
5 cm (2 in.) white Velcro, 2.5 cm (1 in.) wide
Sequins or hot stones

DAISY CHAIN

Artificial daisies or other small flowers
Beading needle and shirring elastic
Small packet green seed beads
Hair grips, if needed

WAND

Approx. 3 m (3¼ yd) ivory, white or pale pink dress net, 5 cm (2 in.) deep
50-cm (20-in.) length of 4 mm (⅛ in.) wooden dowel
Small bag iridescent sequin centres or glitter

JEWELLERY

Pink and white crystals and seed beads (or ready-made necklace and bracelets)
Beige shirring elastic or beading thread for necklace and earrings
Necklace/bracelet fastenings if not using stretch thread

GENERAL EQUIPMENT

Pins, safety pins
Tape measure
Fabric scissors
Small saw
Fine sandpaper or masking or gaffer tape
Protective face mask
White matt spray paint
All-purpose clear adhesive
Clear spray adhesive

Fabric lengths for tutu layers

Size 5
Top layer: 420 x 30 cm (165 x 12 in.)
Middle layer: 348 x 28.5 cm
(137 x 11¼ in.)
Bottom layer: 250 x 27 cm (98½ x 10¾ in.)

Size 6
Top layer: 420 x 34 cm (165 x 13½ in.)
Middle layer: 348 x 32.5 cm (137 x 12¾ in.)
Bottom layer: 250 x 31 cm
(98½ x 12¼ in.)

Size 7
Top layer: 440 x 38 cm (173 x 15 in.)
Middle layer: 368 x 36.5 cm
(145 x 14½ in.)
Bottom layer: 270 x 35 cm
(106 x 13¾ in.)

Size 8
Top layer: 440 x 42 cm
(173 x 16½ in.)
Middle layer: 368 x 40.5 cm
(145 x 16 in.)
Bottom layer: 270 x 39 cm
(106 x 15½ in.)

Basque and tutu

1 Cut out the basque pieces from two layers of white or ivory net.

2 Pin the layers together with the pattern behind, and mark each row (A, B and C) by tacking.

3 For the tutu, cut three lengths of white or ivory dress net to the lengths shown in the box, left.

4 From pink dress net, cut three pieces the same lengths as the tutu layers and 6 cm (2½ in.) deep. Pin the scallop pattern on top and cut out scallops along the edge. Repeat until the scallops run the length of each piece.

Useful Tip

The tutu will fall better if the net is cut on the width, but it may be quicker to cut it on the length to avoid joins.

5 Machine straight stitch a pink scallop-edged net strip along the bottom of each layer of white net so that the scallops are just outside the edges of the white net.

6 Gather the top edge of each white layer (see page 13), so that each layer is the right length to fit on the basque. Secure the ends of the gathering threads with knots.

7 Machine stitch each layer of gathered net to the corresponding tacked line on the net basque, with a double row of stitching on top of the gathering lines. Apply rows B and C with the net facing upwards

(and the seam facing allowance downwards) and row A with the net facing downwards (and the seam allowance facing upwards).

8 Cut out as many petals as you need to fit right around the basque; depending on the size of the child you will probably need around 25 petals. For each petal, you will need two pieces from pink net and one from pink or white glitter net. Join the layers together either by sewing them together with sequins or by fusing them together with hot stones.

9 Pin the petals just above the top (Row A) layer on the net basque, 5 mm (¼ in.) apart, and machine stitch in place.

10 Cut the waistband from yellow stretch velvet or Spandex.

11 To make the tutu removable, pin and machine stitch pieces of yellow loop Velcro to the inside of the waistband at the centre front, sides and centre back.

12 Fold the waistband in half, right sides together. Machine stitch the short ends. Turn the waistband right side out. With right sides together, aligning the raw edges, pin one long side of the waistband to the top of the basque along Row A, and machine stitch. Align the inner waistband edge with the inside stitching, pin and hand stitch the waistband down on the inside of basque.

13 Pin and machine stitch pieces of yellow hook Velcro onto the overlap at the back of the waistband.

14 Pin or tack the layers of net loosely together just inside the hem of the tutu, making sure that all the layers of the tutu are straight. Pin the tip of a petal to the edge of the tutu every 10 cm (4 in.). With a knot on the inside, run a loop of double thread, 4 cm (1½ in.) long, through all three layers of tutu net and the petal tip. Take the thread back down and secure. Repeat until you've stitched on all the petals.

Useful Tip

Fit the leotard on the child before you stitch the corresponding Velcro pieces in place.

Leotard and sleeves

1 Cut out the front and back of the leotard from yellow stretch velvet or Spandex, with the stretch going across the width and the pile of the velvet going upwards. With right sides together, using a stretch stitch, machine stitch the back and front together along the shoulder, crotch and side seams. Turn the leotard right side out.

2 Cut out enough small petals from layers of pink glitter net to go around the neck edge (approx. 21). Assemble them in the same way as the long skirt petals.

3 Pin or tack the petals around the raw neck edge, 5 mm (¼ in.) apart.

4 Cut a strip of stretch velvet long enough for the neck binding and about 4 cm (1½ in.) deep. With right sides together, pin and tack the binding around the neck edge. Machine stitch, using a stretch stitch, trapping the petals in with the neck-binding seam. Fold the raw edge of the binding over to the inside, turn under the raw edge and stitch all around with a stretch stitch or herringbone stitch to retain the stretch in the fabric.

5 Bind the leg openings the same way.

6 Cut the two sleeve pieces from white crystal organza.

7 Cut out enough small petals from pink glitter net to go around the cuffs of each sleeve (approx. 18 per sleeve). Make up same way as for the neck petals. Pin and tack the petals along the cuff edges, 1.5 cm (¾ in.) apart.

Speedy Shortcut

Buy a ready-made leotard. For the right armhole size to fit the sleeve onto, get one with short sleeves.

8 Gather the sleeve heads, as marked on the pattern (see page 15). Pull the back threads to gather the stitching to the required finished length. Secure the ends of the gathering threads with knots.

9 Machine stitch the underarm sleeve seams.

10 Cut two bias strips of white organza (or use bought bias binding) the same length as the sleeve width at the hem and 3 cm (1¼ in.) wide. Pin each bias strip across the inside of the sleeve, as marked on the pattern, trapping the petals in between, and machine topstitch along each edge to form a casing for the elastic.

11 Using a safety pin, feed a 22-cm (8½-in.) length of white 5-mm (¼-in.) elastic through each cuff casing. Hand stitch the ends of the elastic together.

12 With right sides together, aligning the underarm seams with the side seams and the centre of the sleeve head with the shoulder seam, pin the sleeves into the armholes. Machine stitch, using stretch stitch. Clip the curved seams.

13 By hand, stitch three or four daisies down the centre front of the leotard.

Fitting

Fit the tutu on the child over the leotard. Using safety pins, pin the waistband of the tutu onto the leotard slightly below waist level. Check that the waistband is level (see the line on the leotard pattern), then stitch the waistband in place, using a herringbone stitch so that it will stretch (see pages 11 and 14). If you want the tutu to be removable, hand stitch pieces of hook Velcro onto the leotard, to correspond with the pieces of loop Velcro stitched onto the waistband.

Useful Tip

If you are using a bought leotard, try it on the child and pin the sleeves where they fit. Cut the leotard sleeves back if they show.

Wings

1 Cut out the wings from three layers of stiff net (or five layers of dress net), with glitter net for the inside and outside layers. Pin and machine stitch the wings together around the edge.

2 Zigzag stitch single strands of stranded nylon boning across the wings in rows, as marked on the pattern.

3 Machine or hand stitch a length of Velcro down the centre back of the wings.

4 Fold the wings back in the centre on either side of the Velcro to make the wings close a little rather than being completely open and flat.

5 Decorate the wings with sequins or hot stones.

6 Machine or hand stitch the corresponding piece of Velcro down the centre back of the leotard, so that the wings can be removed when the leotard needs to be washed. If the wings flop, tack or tag them to the back of the neckline.

Daisy chain

1 Measure the child's head and make a daisy chain long enough to fit comfortably around it by threading artificial daisies onto shirring elastic with green seed beads in between, leaving about 5 cm (2 in.) between the flowers. The chain can be fixed in place on the child's head with hair grips to stop it from falling off.

Wand

1 Fold and pin the net strip for the pom-pom in half four times until it is about 18.5 cm (7 in.) long. Pin all the layers together. Referring to the template, cut out the

spikes. (It is easier to do this by eye than to pin the template to the net and cut around it.)

2 Ruche the fabric along the straight edge (see page 14). The ruched strip should be about 40 cm (15¾ in.) long.

3 Curl the strip around itself and hand stitch in a tight spiral to make a pom-pom, leaving a hole in the centre that is just big enough to take the length of dowel. Hand stitch the ends of the strip together to secure.

4 Using a small saw, cut a length of dowel about 50 cm (20 in.) long. Sandpaper the cut end smooth to make sure there are no splinters; alternatively, wrap a piece of masking or gaffer tape around the cut end.

5 Wearing a mask and working in a well ventilated area, and following the manufacturer's instructions, spray the dowel with white spray paint.

6 Spread the last 2 cm (¾ in.) of the dowel with all-purpose clear adhesive. While the glue is still tacky, push the dowel gently into the centre of the net pom-pom and leave to dry.

7 Working in a well ventilated area and following the manufacturer's instructions, lightly spray the pom-pom and dowel with clear spray adhesive, and immediately sprinkle with glitter.

Tights and shoes

Choose tights and shoes that are suitable for the time of year. If it's summertime, opt for bare legs; in cooler weather, you could use pale green tights to represent daisy stems. Shoes can be anything from delicate ballet flats or Indian embroidered slippers to a pair of 'daisy root' boots for a funkier fairy.

Jewellery

Make little elasticated bracelets and necklaces by threading tiny crystals and iridescent seed beads onto shirring elastic. (Alternatively, you could use ready-made jewellery.)

Fiery Dragon

Although he looks a bit scary, this dragon is quite a friendly type – the kind that would use his fire-breathing skills to keep you warm in the depths of winter rather than to turn you into a pile of cinders. By adapting the shape of the spines, and using a brown fleece fabric for the body suit, you could make a dinosaur such as a Stegosaurus.

You will need

BODY SUIT AND SPINES

Spandex or red stretch satin for body suit
Cotton quilted lining fabric, preferably with cotton on both sides
Red chunky zip to fit
Iron-on interlining for collar
Red Velcro, 4 cm (1½ in.) wide
Lycra for inner tail
Small bag of polystyrene granules
1 m (1 yd) thin string or cord and safety pin
White 6-mm (¼-in.) Fun Foam for spine bases
Lurid green stretch velvet, Spandex or Lycra to cover spines

HEAD

Red Fun Foam for mask
Black Fun Foam for palette
Scraps of white Fun Foam for teeth
Red Funky Foam for horns
Polystyrene or ping-pong ball
Acid green acrylic paint
Black acrylic paint or marker pen
Black or red baseball cap with adjustable back
Black Velcro, 4 cm (1½ in.) wide, to attach mask to baseball cap

CLAWS AND HOOVES

Lime-green Funky Foam for claws
Bright red gloves
Pair of disposable plastic gloves (optional)
Approx. 1.5 m (60 in.) red or green piping cord, tape or ribbon
Red or white Fun Foam for feet
Black elastic, 2.5 cm (1 in.) wide, for stirrups
Bright red school socks (optional)

GENERAL EQUIPMENT

Pins, safety pins
Tape measure
Fabric scissors
Dressmaker's carbon and tracing wheel
Craft knife and cutting mat
Contact adhesive
Hot glue and glue sticks
Double-sided adhesive tape, 1 cm (½ in.) wide
Fine-nibbed pen
Stapler and staples
Pliers

Fabric

I recommend using a Spandex-type fabric for this costume; it's like a heavyweight Lycra with a two-way stretch. (Standard Lycra may be too lightweight.)

Body suit

1 Cut out the front and back pieces and sleeves from Spandex and from one or two layers of quilted lining fabric. Using a dressmaker's tracing wheel and carbon paper or tailor's chalk and a straight-edge, mark out the quilting pattern on the Spandex front, back and sleeves.

2 Working on a flat surface, tack the front, back and sleeve pieces to their corresponding lining pieces.

3 Machine stitch through all layers along the marked quilting lines to create an effect like a ski jacket. Test this on your machine first, using one or two layers.

4 With right sides together, machine stitch the two back pieces together, leaving an opening in the centre back for the zip as marked on the pattern. Insert the zip (see page 12).

5 With right sides together, machine stitch the two front pieces together along the centre front. Machine stitch the front and back together along the shoulder, side and inside leg seams. Turn the body suit right side out.

6 With right sides together, aligning the edges of the darts, pin and machine stitch the darts at the tops of the sleeves. Pin and machine stitch the underarm seam.

7 Turn the sleeves right side out. With right sides together, aligning the underarm seams with the side seams on the body suit, pin and machine stitch the sleeves to the suit.

8 Cut the collar pieces from Spandex and iron-on interlining. Following the manufacturer's instructions, iron the interlining to the inside back of one collar piece, just inside the seam lines.

9 Assemble the collar (see page 16) and turn the collar right side out.

10 Hand stitch a hook Velcro strip to the back of one side of the collar and loop Velcro extending across the other side of the collar to form the fastening. (Alternatively, you could use hook-and-eye fastenings.)

11 With right sides together, pin and stitch the outer edge of the collar to the body suit neckline.

12 Tuck the raw edges of the seam allowances inside the collar. Pin, then slipstitch around the neckline on the inside.

Tail

1 Cut the outer tail and tail stopper from Spandex and the inner tail and tail stopper from Lycra. Mark and quilt the quilting pattern on the Spandex tail, as for the body suit. With right sides together, machine stitch the quilted tail, leaving a gap of about 1 cm (½ in.) at the tip. Machine stitch the Lycra inner tail, using a stretch stitch and stitching right to the tip. Machine stitch the Lycra tail stopper to the circular end of the Lycra inner tail, leaving a gap of about 10 cm (4 in.) through which to fill the inner tail with polystyrene granules.

2 Fill the Lycra tail with polystyrene granules, but don't over-stuff it. Hand stitch the gap between the stopper and the tail closed.

3 Stitch one end of the piece of thin string to the tip of the filled Lycra tail and tie the other end to a safety pin. Feed the safety pin down the Spandex tail and out through the little hole at the end. Pull on the string until the end of the Lycra tail is fully inside the tip of the Spandex tail. Snip the string off through the hole, and sew up the gap by hand on the seam line. Do not attach the tail to the body (just yet). Turn in the seam allowances and slipstitch the Spandex tail stopper to the open end of the tail.

4 Try the body suit on the child to ascertain the hem lengths for the cuffs and legs. Turn under and pin the hems, and slipstitch around.

5 Cut out the tummy pads from two layers of quilted lining fabric. Slipstitch the pads to the lining of the suit to create the rounded tummy shape.

Useful Tip

To get around the fact that the zip is in the very centre of the back, position the spines as close to the zip as you can without preventing it from moving up and down. Sew around one side of the cover only, leaving the other side to sit over the zip, but not actually attached. Place the spines on alternate sides of the zip, which gives the impression that they are all in the centre. Continue in this way after the zip has ended; it gives it more character than placing the spines in a straight, orderly line.

Spines

1 Using a craft knife on a cutting mat, cut out the spine bases from Fun Foam. Bevel the spine side edges (not the base), so that they glue together more easily.

2 Apply contact adhesive (see page 8) along the long edges of all the spines and leave until touch dry. Bond together, edge to edge.

3 Cut out the spine covers from green stretch velvet, Spandex or Lycra. With right sides together, pin and machine stitch the seams, using a stretch stitch. (If the material slides too much, tack it before machining.) Trim the seam allowances and points and turn the spine covers right side out.

4 Insert the Fun Foam spine bases into the covers. There is no need to glue them in place, as they will be sewn onto the spine of the suit, which will keep them firmly in place.

5 Try the costume on the child to check the tail position, before you attach the spines. Following the template, pin the spines along the centre back from the neck right down to the end of the tail, starting at the top with the biggest spines and finishing with the smallest ones at the end of the tail. It is important to tension the spine covers tightly, turning the seam allowance under around the base. This will help them to stand upright without wobbling.

Attaching the tail

1 Pad out the body suit with a cushion to make a firm base to sew the tail onto. Pin the tail to the suit, keeping the tension of the suit underneath the tail taut, and slipstitch it securely in place.

Head

1 Using a craft knife on a cutting mat, cut out the head front and sides from red Fun Foam. Cut the edges of the side panels at an angle of 45° and mark a notch on each side, as marked on the pattern. Apply contact adhesive around the edges and leave until the glue is touch dry. Glue the pieces together, edge to edge, matching the notches.

2 Cut out the palette and teeth from black and white Fun Foam respectively. Glue the teeth to the palette.

3 Glue the palette into the inside of the jaw.

4 Following the pattern, cut the eyelids and nostrils from red Fun Foam. Glue them in place on the front of the head.

5 Cut out the ears from red Fun Foam. Cut along the dart lines, as marked on the pattern, and glue the edges together so that the ears are curved. Glue two red Funky Foam whiskers to each ear, then glue the ears to the head, using hot or cool melt glue.

Horns

1 Cut two 82 x 4-cm (32¼ x 1½-in.) strips of red Funky Foam. (Zigazg stitch strips together on the sewing machine if necessary to get a piece that is long enough.)

2 Cut the corner off one end of each piece, as shown on the pattern. This is the end that you start rolling. Place a strip of 1-cm (½-in.) double-sided tape along one edge of the strip and peel off the protective paper. Start rolling evenly and tightly, at an angle of about 45°, gently easing the strip into a slight curve.

3 When you reach the end, either sew a couple of stitches or use fine tags to hold the spiral in place and stop it from unwinding. Triim the end flush.

4 Cut out the end stoppers for the horns from Fun Foam and glue them into the ends of the horns to give them a solid base. Check the angle of the horns on the head, then glue the horns in place, using contact adhesive or hot or cool melt glue.

Useful Tip

If you can't find foam the right colour, apply a thin coat of contact adhesive to white foam as a primer. When the glue is dry, paint the foam with acrylic paint.

Attaching the head spines

1 First, mark out the positions of the head spines. The spines become smaller as they go down the nose.

2 Glue the seam allowance of the covering fabric under the spine bases. Draw around the base of each spine in position on the head. Apply hot or cool melt glue to either the head and the base of the spines, and glue the spines to the head.

Eyes

1 Cut a polystyrene ball or ping-pong ball in half. Paint each half with acid green acrylic paint. Leave to dry.

2 Draw around the slit pupil template using a fine-nibbed pen, then fill it in using black acrylic paint or a black marker pen. For a scarier look, go for a narrow slit; a broader pupil looks friendlier. Make sure both eyes are looking in the same direction.

3 Glue the eyeballs into the eye sockets. (If using hot glue, apply glue to the eye socket and allow to cool a little before you insert the eyeball, to avoid melting).

Attaching the head

1 Cut the peak off a black or red baseball hat with an adjustable strap at the back.

2 Stitch a piece of loop Velcro across the top of the cap in the centre.

3 Using contact adhesive, glue the corresponding piece of hook Velcro into the top of the head.

Claws

1 Cut ten 42 x 2-cm (16½ x ¾-in.) strips of green Funky Foam for the claws. Cut the corner off one end, as shown on the pattern. (This is the same process as making the horns.)

2 Place a strip of 1-cm (½-in.) double-sided tape along one long edge of the foam and peel off the protective paper. Start rolling tightly at an angle of about 45°. When you reach the end, staple to secure. Flatten the staples with pliers to prevent them from scratching.

3 Get the child to put on a pair of red gloves, then slide each claw over one finger end to see how far the claws slide down. Using contact adhesive, glue the claws in place with the child still wearing the gloves. (The glue should not soak right through, but a pair of disposable plastic gloves could be worn underneath, just in case.) Alternatively, the claws could simply be jammed straight onto the ends of the fingers and secured with a little double-sided tape, but they will probably fall off and get lost, so make some spares.

4 Attach a length of red or green piping cord, tape or ribbon to one of the glove cuffs. Thread the tape up the sleeve, through the body, and down the other sleeve, and attach it to the other glove so the gloves dangle outside the sleeves and can be taken off when not in use.

Hooves

1 Check the paper pattern over the shoes to make sure the pieces will fit. Adjust the pattern if necessary.

2 Cut out the feet pieces from red or white Fun Foam and glue them together along the centre backs and centre fronts using contact adhesive. Butt join the central claw and side claws to the base of the front of the foot, as marked on the pattern.

3 Glue a piece of 2.5-cm (1-in.) elastic under the instep as a stirrup. Wear over rubber-soled soft shoes, with red school socks.

Useful Tip

Make sure the Velcro inside the head aligns with te Velcro on the baseball hat.

ghoulish ghost

At Halloween, when scary monsters, ghouls and other things that go bump in the night come out to play, you may catch a glimpse of this spooky-eyed figure swathed in a misty grey veil and robe, underneath which can be glimpsed a bony skeleton that glows in the dark. Be afraid – be very afraid!

You will need

SKELETON SUIT

Fun Foam for skeleton
Glow-in-the-dark paint (optional)
Black all-in-one unitard with a high or polo neck and a zip down the back
Polythene bags for stuffing suit
Plastic food wrap

ROBE AND VEIL

Grey silk, polyester georgette or crystal chiffon for robe and veil
Net or crystal chiffon for robe's under layer and veil
Approx. 1 m (1 yd) black cord or millinery elastic, 1 cm (1/2 in.) wide, for drawstring at neck
Fusible bonding web to attach eyes
Spooky holographic fabric for eyes
Black Funky Foam to back eyes (optional)

FABRIC DYEING (OPTIONAL)

Black fabric dye
Table salt as specified by dye manufacturer

Large cheap saucepan for hot dye, or washing-up bowl or plastic bucket for cold dye
Wooden laundry tongs for lifting dyed fabric out of container
Wooden spoons for stirring dye
Disposable or rubber gloves
Trouser hangers with clips at either end

HEADDRESS

White hook Velcro, 2.5 cm (1 in.) wide, to attach veil to headdress frame
10 cm (4 in.) black loop Velcro to attach headdress frame to centre of veil
Small narrow lampshade frame between 10 and 15 cm (4 and 6 in.) high, and head width or narrower
Plain black beanie hat
Flat-based LED light (they usually have hook Velcro on them; if not, stick a self-adhesive Velcro tab onto the base)
10 cm (4 in.) black loop Velcro, 2.5 cm (1 in.) wide, to attach LED light

GENERAL EQUIPMENT

Pins
Fabric scissors
Tape measure
Fine-tipped marker pen
Craft knife and cutting mat
Medium-grade sandpaper (optional)
Tailor's chalk or safety pins
Polythene sheeting or plastic bags
Contact adhesive
Talcum powder
Pinking shears
Non-stick silicone baking paper
Double-sided carpet tape

Skeleton suit

1 Place the pattern pieces on the Fun Foam and trace around the outline with a fine-tipped marker pen.

2 Using a craft knife on a cutting mat, cut out the bones, making sure you cut out a right and a left of all bones of which there are two. Sandpaper any rough edges. Paint the bones with glow-in-the-dark paint (optional), but test first.

3 Dress the child in the unitard. Using tailor's chalk, mark where the bones should go, keeping the joints free so that they can still bend.

4 Take the unitard off the child. Stuff the unitard with polythene sheeting and bags, or even inflated beach balls, so that it looks as if someone is wearing it. Alternatively, trace around your child on flat cardboard, cut out, cover the cardboard with plastic food wrap and dress it in the unitard.

5 Apply contact adhesive (see page 8) to the backs of the bones. While the glue is wet, use the bones as a stamp to imprint glue on the right place on the unitard. If the glue soaks through, the fabric should still peel off the polythene fairly easily when you un-stuff it. Leave until the glue is touch dry, then bond the bones to the unitard. Remove the stuffing and dust the inside of the unitard with talcum powder.

Speedy Shortcut

Buy a painted skeleton suit, available from fancy-dress suppliers.

Useful Tip

Fun Foam is fairly resistant to paint. You may need to spread a very thin coat of contact adhesive over all the bones as a key, and leave it to dry thoroughly before you apply the glow-in-the-dark paint. Use polythene to stuff the unitard, as some other plastics might stick.

Preparing the fabric for dyeing (optional)

Shading the hems of both the robe and the veil so that they blend to black creates a really dramatic effect. If you are planning to do this, buy extra fabric to allow for shrinkage and pre-shrink the fabrics before you cut out the pieces, by wetting, drying and ironing. Minimise ironing by folding and hanging the fabric flat to dry. Do not tumble dry without testing a piece first, as the fabric may thicken and lose its translucent quality.

Robe and veil

1 Using pinking shears, cut out all the pieces for both the top fabric and the under layer.

2 Machine stitch the top-fabric and under layer panels for the robe together separately to form two circles.

3 With right sides together, pin and tack the top layer and under layer around the neckline, then machine stitch. Turn right side out, press and topstitch close to the edge.

4 Topstitch a second row of stitching around the neckline 1 cm (½ in.) from the first, to form a channel. Thread millinery elastic through the channel to form a drawstring.

5 Check the hem is not too long at the front.

6 Repeat steps 1 and 2 to make the veil. Do not stitch the veil top layer and under layer together, but pin it in the centre.

Dyeing the robe and veil

1 Test a small piece of the fabric to see how quickly the dye takes. (Note that polyester and acetate fabrics do not dye.) Rinse and dry the test piece to assess the depth of colour, as fabric looks darker when wet.

2 Following the dye manufacturer's instructions, prepare a large saucepan of black or dark dye (you can use up old dyes to make a dark colour).

3 Fold and clip the tops of the robe and veil to trouser hangers. The wet fabric will be very heavy.

4 Wet the costume completely in the bath, then remove. Leave 10 cm (4 in.) of water in the bath.

5 Carefully place the saucepan of dye in the bath directly under the shower head. Holding the hanger, dunk the hem of the wet costume into the dye pot. As the fabric is wet, there should not be a hard line where the dye stops. Pull the fabric out, allowing the lowest 15 cm (6 in.) or so to remain in the dye to obtain a deeper shade.

6 Once you have the right shade, take the fabric out of the dye pot and dunk it in the shallow water in the bath to remove most of the dye. The rest can be removed by rinsing the fabric under the shower.

7 Hang the fabric up on the shower head rail or, better still, outside on a washing line.

Useful Tip

If you do not have the right hangers, safety pin the costume sections to a regular strong wire or wooden hanger.

Eyes

1 Following the manufacturer's instructions, apply fusible bonding web to the back of the holographic fabric. Cut out the eye shapes and iron them in position onto the veil.

2 Cut out the same eye shapes from black Funky Foam. Using contact adhesive, stick the foam shapes behind the eyes to support them (optional).

3 Lay the veil directly on top of the under layer and tack them together at the centre point. Hand stitch a circle or a tab of hook Velcro in the centre of the circle on the inside, stitching through both layers

Headdress

1 Stitch a circle of loop Velcro to the top of the lampshade frame and a circle of loop Velcro to the top of the beanie hat.

2 Put the beanie hat on the child, place the lampshade frame on top to check the position on the child's head and mark with chalk or safety pins. Stitch the lampshade frame securely to the beanie hat.

3 Stick a hook Velcro circle to the back of the LED light and a loop Velcro circle to the top of the beanie hat. Aligning the pieces of Velcro, attach the LED light to the top of the beanie hat and the head veil to the top of the lampshade.

4 Make sure that the child can see through the veil. If necessary, cut a panel out of one or both layers at eye level.

Little Devil

Dressed in this costume, this Little Devil can get up to all the mischief he likes! The black and red colour combination really conjures up images of fire and brimstone and is perfect for 'trick or treat' at Halloween. Like Mervin the Martian on page 56, the base for this costume is a ready-made scoop-necked unitard – in this case, bright red. I dyed the arms and legs black up to the waist for a more sinister look.

You will need

BODY SUIT

Two-way stretch bright red Lycra (for balaclava and cowl, if needed)
Red Velcro for back of balaclava (and cowl, if needed)
All-over nylon Lycra unitard (see below)
Black dustbin liners for hairy texture
Approx. 4 m (4¼ yd) black or brown cotton muslin or fine turban cotton
Black acrylic hair switch to add into the hair texture pieces (optional)

WINGS

2 x A3 sheets of black Funky Foam
Approx. 3 m (3¼ yd) stranded nylon boning, narrow or wide width
10 cm (4 in.) black Velcro, 5 cm (2 in.) wide

TAIL, TRIDENT, EARS, HORNS AND HOOVES

Red insulating tape
Approx. 22 x 30 ml chemical measuring cups
Matt black spray paint, or black acrylic paint and small sponge to apply
Large black or pewter jeweller's headpins, as long as possible
Black Fun Foam for tail, trident and hooves
Red Funky Foam for horns and ears
Black elastic, 2.5 cm (1 in.) wide, for stirrups of hooves

GENERAL EQUIPMENT

Pins
Tape measure
Fabric scissors
Black fabric dye and basic dyeing equipment (optional)
PVA adhesive to glue gathering knots
Tailor's chalk or marker pen
Fine tagging gun and tags
All-purpose clear adhesive or hot glue gun and glue sticks
Plastic sheet
Disposable plastic gloves
Punch pliers, or thick pin or needle and lighter
Craft knife and cutting mat
Fine-nosed pliers
Contact adhesive
Double-sided adhesive tape 1 cm (½ in.) wide

unitard options

Choose from a full cat suit with balaclava (which you may have to get specially made), a high-necked unitard with a zip up the back (you will have to make the balaclava), or a scoop-necked unitard (you will need to make a balaclava and cowl). Alternatively, opt for cotton leggings, a long-sleeved T-shirt and a beanie hat.

Balaclava and cowl (if required)

1 Cut out the balaclava sides and centre panels and the cowl pieces from red Lycra. (You will need an inner and an outer layer, both cut from Lycra.)

2 Tack or pin and, using a stretch stitch, machine stitch the panels for the outer and inner balaclavas together separately (see page 21), leaving an opening in both centre backs for the Velcro as marked on the pattern.

3 Place the inner and outer balaclavas right sides together. Using a stretch stitch, machine stitch around the face opening and turn right side out. Topstitch around the face opening by machine to keep the layers together.

4 Tack the open edges together around the outside and centre back edges, then zigzag both layers together. Remove the tacking stitches.

5 Assemble the cowl (see step 5, page 21). Machine stitch the balaclava onto the cowl around the neck.

6 Insert the Velcro in the centre back seam.

7 Try the unitard and balaclava on the child and mark where the cowl overlaps the unitard. Join the cowl to the neckline of the unitard. Pin or tack and topstitch using a stretch stitch.

Body suit texture

This technique makes a great alternative to bland fur fabric. I used black bin bags and cotton muslin, cut into strips and ruched to make an interesting texture, but either material can be used on its own. If you can't find black or brown cotton muslin, dye the fabric or dip it in strong tea. A patchy finish is better than an even, flat one.

1 Cut strips 10–12 cm (4–5 in.) wide from the bin bags along the length of the bag, and open up into a double strip. Cutting through several layers at once, cut muslin strips the same width across the width of the fabric.

2 Cut short lengths of the black acrylic hair a little longer than the width of the bin bag and muslin strips. Set the hair to one side until you have finished ruching the strips.

3 Ruche one long edge of the strips by using a large glass-headed pin to make tiny pleats (see page 14).

4 Zigzag stitch the lengths of acrylic hair to the top long edge of the ruched strips of muslin every 8 to 10 cm (3 or 4 in.) or so, then put a few blobs of PVA adhesive over the stitching to stop the hair from falling out. Make approx. 30 strips, depending on the size of the child and the width of the fabric.

5 Make the edges jagged, by bunching up the material and roughly cutting through the bottom long edges of the strips. Try the unitard on the child and mark horizontal lines on the lower part of the unitard to show where to place the strips, approx. 8–10 cm (3–4 in.) apart, using tailor's chalk or a marker pen. The lines should go from mid calf to just below the waist.

6 Take the unitard off and, using a fine tagging gun or a needle and thread and working upwards, attach the top edge of the strips to the unitard every 4 cm (1½ in.) or so, leaving a gap of about 4 cm (1½ in.) before

> ### Useful Tip
>
> Instead of muslin for the body suit texture, you could use fine turban cotton available only in certain shops and markets. It comes in every colour and is even cheaper than muslin.

> ### Useful Tip
>
> Check the pattern of the cowl against the neckline of the unitard before you cut out the cowl pieces. The cowl can overlap the neckline of the unitard, so it does not have to match it exactly.

Useful Tip

Tag the strips on loosely to avoid losing the stretch in the Lycra (remember that the Lycra has to stretch over the child's legs; if you are using a needle and thread and have the time, use a herringbone stitch or catch the fabric every 4 cm (1½ in.), taking care not to gather the Lycra.

starting the next strip, to retain the stretch in the fabric. Alternate between muslin strips and strips of bin bag. The texture will fill in any gaps, particularly if the background is dark.

Wings

1 Cut out both wing shapes from black Funky Foam and zigzag stitch them together at the centre back, as marked on the pattern.

2 Separate the nylon boning into individual strands by cutting down the centre of the strip, taking one half, holding the long threads and nylon strands together at the top, and stripping the selvedge and crossways threads away from the nylon strands.

3 Zigzag stitch strands of boning across both wings, as indicated on the pattern, to form fine 'bones' that will stop the wings from flopping.

Useful Tip

If the threads of the nylon boning get tangled up when you are trying to separate them, cut them free and proceed until you have single nylon filaments like stiff fishing wire.

4 Backstitch at the filament ends and put a blob of all-purpose clear adhesive on each exposed end.

5 Sew four lengths of un-stripped boning as 'bones' at the centre back, as indicated on the pattern.

6 Sew a 5-cm (2-in.) piece of hook Velcro in the centre of the centre back, over the 'bones'. This will attach to the loop half of the Velcro, which needs to be sewn onto the centre back of the unitard – at the back of the cowl, or partly on the unitard (depending on the costume).

Tail

1 Wind red insulating tape diagonally around each measuring cup until the cup is fully covered. You do not need to cover the bases. Trim off any excess.

2 Shading each section of the tail is optional. Place the cups on a plastic sheet to protect your work surface. Wearing disposable gloves, spray the upper half of the cups with matt black spray paint, avoiding making a hard line. Leave until completely dry.

Useful Tip

Do not be tempted to use plastic shots glasses in place of the chemical measuring cups, as they shatter.

Useful Tips

Do not spray the cups without covering them first with insulating tape, as the paint will fall off in large flakes.

Spray from a distance of approx. 30 cm (12 in.), as this gives you better control of the paint and it is less likely to run.

Test the paint adherence before spraying. If spray paint does not stick, try applying acrylic paint with a small sponge, fading it out the edges. Failing that, stipple on colour with a large black marker pen.

3 Using punch pliers set to the smallest hole, make one hole at the top and one at the bottom of each cup, on opposite sides, approx. 5 mm (1/4-in.) from the edge. Make sure that the holes are directly opposite each other and that the holes are no bigger than the headpins or they will fall through.

4 Glue thin wisps of black acrylic hair to the top of each cup, one wisp on either side, using either hot or cool melt glue or all-purpose clear adhesive, before linking the cups together.

5 Using a craft knife, cut the base out of one cup only. Punch sewing holes around the base, far enough in not to tear when you pull the thread. This will be the first cup in the tail.

6 Link the cups together by threading the headpins through from the wide end of one cup to the narrow (base) end of the next cup, straight through the cup and out the other side. If necessary, using fine-nosed pliers, make small loops at both ends of the headpins to stop them from falling back through the holes.

7 Sew the base of the first cup to the back of the unitard. Position the tail below the waist, but high enough for the child to be able to sit down.

Trident

1 Cut out two trident shapes for the end of the tail from black Fun Foam. Chamfer the long edges to 45° and glue the pieces together with contact adhesive (see page 8), leaving the short end open.

2 Pinch the pieces apart and clamp the trident over the last cup on the tail; if it does not fit tightly, glue it in place with hot or cool melt glue.

Horns

1 Cut one strip of red Funky Foam for each horn, using the pattern. (Zigzag-stitch pieces together on the sewing machine if necessary to get a long enough strip.)

2 Cut the corner off one end of each piece, as shown on the pattern. This is the end that you start rolling. Place a strip of 1-cm (1/2-in.) double-sided tape along one

edge of the strip. peel off the protective paper and roll at an angle of 45°, easing it into a slight curve.

3 When you reach the end, sew a couple of stitches or use staples (squashed flat with pliers) to hold the spiral in place and stop it unwinding. Trim the end flush.

4 Cut a foam disk to the inside diameter of the hollow base. Apply contact adhesive around the edge of the disk and the inside edge of the horn, and leave until touch dry. Insert the foam disk into the base of the horn to form a flat base.

5 Position the horns on the balaclava, check the angle of the horns on the head, and glue in place with contact adhesive.

Ears

1 Cut out a left and right ear from red Funky Foam, curve the base round in a U-shape, and stitch them to the balaclava as indicated on the pattern.

Cloven hooves

1 Cut out the hoof pieces from black Fun Foam or Funky Foam.

2 If you are using Fun Foam, cut the fronts at an angle, as on the pattern. Using contact adhesive, glue the angled edges together, edge to edge. Glue the rest of the centre front and centre back seams together, edge to edge. Funky Foam can be zigzagged edge to edge or overlapped and topstitched on the sewing machine.

3 Check that the opening is big enough for the child's foot. If it is not, trim away some of the foam. Sew or glue a black elastic stirrup under the instep.

Useful Tips

If you do not have punch pliers. hold a thick needle or large glass-headed pin in fine-nosed pliers and heat it with a lighter.

Make sure the headpins are long enough to go through both holes. leaving enough at both ends to form a loop. If the headpins can be pulled through the holes. even after you have formed an extra loop, thread on wide. flat beads to act as washers.

Do not pull the headpins too tight; the tail should be loose and floppy. like a hinged toy snake or a dustbin rubble shoot on a building site.

Pegleg the Pirate

Ahoy, me hearties! Laden with jewels and other loot, this swashbuckling buccaneer is ready to roam the high seas in search of treasure. Small, seemingly insignificant, details can make a big difference to a costume. Pirates are generally a scruffy, motley crew who care little for either fashion or personal hygiene, so Pegleg's shirt has been aged and stained by dipping it in cold tea, while his buttons are an odd assortment that he probably cut off the clothes of his hapless victims! Always think about the kind of life your character would lead and embellish and accessorise the costume accordingly.

You will need

TROUSERS

Dark red panne velvet or loose-weave fine wool
Approx. 75 cm (30 in.) black elastic, 2 cm (¾ in.) wide
Approx. 75 cm (30 in.) black elastic, 6 mm (¼ in.) wide

SHIRT

Fine white or cream cotton
Strong tea

WAISTCOAT

Loose-woven textured fabric such as a rough linen
Approx. 3 m (3¼ yd) burgundy bias binding, 1 cm (½ in.) wide
Approx. 25 cm (10 in.) Velcro, 4 cm (1½ in.) wide, for front fastening
6 x vintage metal buttons in different designs and sizes

SASH

1 m (1 yd) each of two striped cotton fabrics in rich colours
1 m (1 yd) gold fabric, woven not knits
Velcro tabs or hook-and-eye fasteners

BOOT COVERS

Pair of cheap Wellington boots
Brown felt (wool or wool viscose mix)
Black elastic, 2 cm (¾ in.) wide, for stirrups
Black heavyweight iron-on interlining for boot cuff
Non-stick silicone baking paper

THREE-CORNERED HAT AND HAIR

Hair pieces or 'wefting'
Basic brown or black child's felt hat with wide brim and a round crown
Strip of fabric torn from the sash for the edge of the hat
1 ostrich feather
1 decorative button
Assorted beads to string in hair
Beading thread
1 m (1 yd) red ribbon or a torn strip of a lightweight red cotton or silk

GENERAL EQUIPMENT

Pins, safety pins
Tape measure
Fabric scissors
Yarn, string or leather thonging

Trousers

1 Cut out the trouser fronts and backs from panne velvet or loose-weave fine wool. With right sides together, machine stitch the inside leg seams. With right sides together, machine stitch the crotch seams together.

2 Turn under along the fold line at the top of the waist and topstitch to form a channel 3 cm (1¼ in.) deep, leaving an opening at one side seam through which to thread the elastic.

3 Attach a safety pin to one end of a length of 2-cm- (¾-in.)-wide elastic and feed the elastic through the channel. Hand stitch the ends of the elastic together.

4 Turn up the hems and pin and topstitch to form a narrow casing. Attach a length of narrow elastic to a bodkin or safety pin, thread the elastic through the casing and hand stitch the ends of the elastic together.

5 Turn the trousers right side out. If necessary, machine stitch elastic braces at the front of the trousers, cross them over at the back and machine or hand stitch at the back after checking the length on the child.

Shirt

1 To age the shirt, dip the fabric in a very strong tea mixture to age it; if it comes out patchy, so much the better! Hang the fabric up to dry to minimise ironing.

Useful Tip

Ageing the shirt is optional, but it adds a touch of authenticity. Remember, however, that this process may shrink the fabric – so allow for a little more fabric than you will need and age the fabric before you cut out the pattern pieces.

2 Cut out the front, back, sleeves, collar and front facing from the dipped fabric.

3 Cut a slit in the centre front and facing, as marked on the pattern. With right sides together, machine stitch on either side of the slit in a closed V-shape, turn right side out and press. With right sides together, machine stitch the front and back together along the side and shoulder seams.

4 Set the stitch length to its longest setting and machine stitch two parallel rows of stitching 5 mm (¼ in.) apart around the sleeve heads, as indicated on the pattern.

5 With right sides together, machine stitch the underarm seams and press the seams flat.

6 With right sides together, machine stitch the sides of the undercuffs and press flat.

7 Align the undercuff with the sleeve and match up the topstitching lines on the patterns. Sew two rows of topstitching to form a casing, leaving a small opening to insert the elastic.

8 Using a safety pin, feed narrow elastic through the casings. Hand stitch the ends of the elastic together.

9 Pull the back threads to gather the sleeve heads until they fit the armholes exactly.

10 With right sides together, aligning the underarm seams with the side seams and the centre of the sleeve head with the shoulder seam, pin and machine stitch the sleeves into the armholes. Clip the curved seams.

11 Fold the collar in half lengthways, right sides together. Machine stitch along the outside and short edges. Turn right side out, trim the corners and press. Attach the collar to the shirt (see page 17).

12 Cut a 60 x 3.5-cm (24 x 1³⁄₈-in.) strip of the shirt fabric for the ties. Fold it in half, right sides together, and machine stitch along the long, raw edge to form a tube. Attach a safety pin to one end of the tube, then feed the safety pin through the tube so that it pulls the fabric back on itself and turns the tube right side out.

Useful Tip

The waistcoat facings can be made from the same fabric as the top fabric, or from a fabric in the same colour as the waistcoat binding.

13 Cut the strip in half to make two ties. Hand stitch one tie to the base of the collar on each side. The ties look better just hanging, not done up; really cool pirates should look somewhat dishevelled!

14 If you prefer a rough, weathered look for your costume, make a few holes in the fabric and fray the edges of the shirt.

Waistcoat

1 Cut out the front and back pieces and the front and back facings.

2 Bind the bottom edge of the back waistcoat piece (see page 18).

3 With right sides together, pin and machine stitch the fronts to the back along the shoulder and side seams.

4 Machine stitch the front and back facings together along the shoulder seams.

5 With right sides together, pin the facings to the waistcoat along the neck edge and down the centre fronts and hems. Clip the corners, turn right side out and press.

6 Bind the armholes, front hem and sides to meet the back waistcoat.

7 Cut a strip of Velcro and machine stitch it to the centre fronts, with one half on the inside and the other on the outside, as marked on the pattern. Hand stitch six buttons to the right front of the waistcoat.

Sash

1 Rip the fabrics into strips, making two of the strips slightly longer than the child's waist measurement and about 40 cm (16 in.) deep, and the third one about 50 cm (20 in.) deep and long enough to hang to around mid-calf length.

2 Attach Velcro or hook-and-eye fasteners to the ends of the two shorter strips so that they can be fastened around the child's waist.

3 Twist and tie the third strip around the child's waist at the side, leaving one end hanging down to around knee level and one to mid-calf level.

4 Fray the ends of the third strip to make a fringe.

Boot covers

1 Cut out the boot cover sides and centre pieces from brown felt. (Check the size of the paper pattern against the Wellington boots before you cut the pieces out.) Machine stitch the seams. Clip the curved seams, open up and topstitch on either side of the seam line using a zigzag stitch.

Buttons

Find some interesting old buttons, preferably metal. If they're different designs and sizes, this will add character. Think about the history of the pirate – what he has looted and pillaged in his chequered past, and where he may have come across his buttons!

Antique pleating (optional)

For a great textural look, wet the sash fabric and twist it from either end as tightly as possible, until the fabric twists back on itself into a spiral. (Get someone to help you if possible.) Attach a big safety pin to both ends, or tie the ends together with string to keep the fabric from unravelling, and hang the fabric up to dry. When it is completely dry, undo the string or safety pin: the fabric will unravel into a wonderfully crinkled texture.

2 Machine or hand stitch one side of the elastic stirrup under the sole of the boot covers.

3 To cover the boots, pull the boot cover over the top of the boot. You may need to pinch the boot top to get the ankle part of the cover through, as this will be narrower. It should be a tight fit without buckling the boot. Hand stitch the other side of the elastic stirrup in place.

4 Cut out the cuff pattern from felt and from iron-on interlining. Following the manufacturer's instructions, iron the interlining to the felt cuff, just inside the seam allowance of the felt.

5 Turn the edges of the felt over the interlining edges all the way around, and topstitch a double row of straight or zigzag stitches to finish.

6 Fold the seam allowance of the boot cover over to the outside of the boot, then pin the wrong side of the top of the cuff to the edge of the seam line. It is better to do this when the cover is on the boot to keep the shape taut. Make sure that the cuff is centred at the front, so that if there is any discrepancy between the sizes of the cuff and cover, it can be 'lost' at the back of the boot.

7 Whipstitch (see page 10) the top of the boot cover to the cuff by hand along the very top edge, right around the boot top. The ends of the cuff will stick out at the back. They can either be left open or stitched part or all the way down the back.

Three-cornered hat and hair

1 Full wigs are hot and bulky. The hat only needs a fringe of hair around the underside of the brim – leaving a space for the face, of course! Try the hat on the child for size, with the hair loosely attached. Using strong thread, hand stitch the hair to the inside of the hat. (You can stitch right through to the outside of the hat; it will not show.)

2 Mark the brim at three points – the centre of the forehead and behind each ear – so that it is divided into three equal-sized sections. Sew the brim to the crown in the centre of each point, using big stitches of yarn, string or leather thonging, to create a three-cornered or 'tricorne' hat.

3 Hand stitch the strip of torn sash fabric around the very edge of the brim and allow it to fray.

4 Sew the ostrich feather inside the brim, pointing backwards, and sew or hot glue a button over the quill at the base of the feather.

5 String the beads or use ready-strung beads and stitch them to the underside of the hat brim, hanging down, where the brim meets the hair. Tie one side of the hair with red ribbon, cotton or silk

Adapting an adult-sized hat

If you are adapting an adult-sized felt hat that is too big, cut the crown off the hat approx. 1 cm (½ in.) above the brim. Cut it down further, parallel to this, if it is still too deep. Overlap the brim and the crown and re-stitch the brim to the crown by hand, using fairly big stitches.

Accessories

Pirates need to show off all the loot that they have plundered on the high seas! Find or buy an assortment of beads to put around Pegleg's neck. I found a selection of cheap ethnic necklaces in my local market and put a couple around his neck, and another around his waist over the sash.

Add any cheap rings the right size, along with a magnetic earring (or a hoop that that will simply hang over his ear).

Marina the Mermaid

Made in shades of green and azure blue, this little mermaid's costume has a real feel of the sea about it. A 'seaweed' boa makes a lovely finishing touch.

This is a great recycling project: old polythene bags and dust sheets are used for the tail, green bubble wrap for the seaweed boa, and coloured plastic bottles for the fish 'scales' on the skirt. If you want something longer lasting than polythene for the frills, opt for white, blue or green crystal organza and cut the fabric with pinking shears to minimise fraying. Dress net is another option that does not fray.

You will need

SKIRT, BOLERO TOP AND FRILLS

Blue-green Spandex and/or nylon
  Lycra for skirt and bolero top
Sturdy zip to fit
Brown, green and blue plastic bottles
  for making scales
White, pale pink or flesh-coloured
  ready-made Lycra leotard
Velcro for bolero fastening
Assorted crystals, hot stones, sequins,
  seed pearls and seed beads for
  decorating bolero
Clear plastic bags or clear polythene
  sheet, 45 micron, for tail fin,
  neckline and wrist strap frills

SEAWEED BOA

Green bubble wrap
Approx. 50 cm (20 in.) white millinery
  elastic
1 string blue-green iridescent cup
  sequins

GENERAL EQUIPMENT

Pins, safety pins
Tape measure
Fabric and general-purpose scissors
Fine-tipped blue or green marker pen
Fine and micro tagging guns and tags
  (optional)
Large pin or needle, for making
  sewing holes in scales
Fine-nosed pliers
Lighter or night light for heating pin to
  make holes
Dressmaker's tracing paper and a
  tracing wheel
Clear adhesive tape
All-purpose clear adhesive
Tailor's chalk
Double-sided adhesive tape (optional)

Fishtail skirt

1 Cut out the skirt from a single layer of Spandex or a double layer of Lycra tacked together. (Spandex is a better weight for the skirt than Lycra.) Pin and tack the centre back seam. Try the skirt on the child to check the fit (it should be a snug fit but not clingy or too tight), and adjust if necessary.

2 Machine stitch the centre back using a stretch stitch, leaving a gap at the base for the zip as marked on the pattern.

3 Insert the zip in the centre back seam (see page 12).

Making scales (optional)

1 Wash the plastic bottles, remove any labels, and dry.

2 Cut out the top and the bottom of the bottles so you are left with a straight cylinder.

3 Cut away and discard any plastic that has glue residue left from the bottle labels.

4 Cut the bottles into horizontal strips the height of the scales that you are cutting. Think 'thumbnails', so that the curve of the bottle goes around the scale, not up and down it. Now cut the strips into small squares the same width as the scales. Draw around the paper patterns with a fine marker pen and cut out. Use the first scale you cut as a new template; it will fit over the curve better and not deteriorate. You should get 40–55 scales per bottle, depending on the size of the bottle and the scale. Do not use your fabric scissors to cut plastic!

5 Hold a large pin or needle with pliers and, using a lighter or night light, heat the needle and pierce the plastic to make a sewing hole at the top of each side of the scale, as marked on the pattern. Work quickly before the needle cools. Alternatively, use the smallest hole on punch pliers to make the sewing holes.

Useful Tips

Do not make holes too close to the edges of the scales or they may break.

I distributed the colours of scales randomly but, provided you have the right number of each colour, you could make repeating patterns, if you like.

Speedy Shortcut

If you do not have time to make the scales, decorate the fishtail skirt with shimmery sequins instead.

Applying the scales

1 Mark the horizontal lines for the scales on the mermaid skirt. Tailor's chalk wears off quickly, so use dressmaker's tracing paper and a tracing wheel, a fine marker pen or tacking stitches in a contrasting colour, such as red. Alternatively, tack or mark the lines by eye, keeping the lines evenly spaced.

2 Roll the top of the skirt down into a roll, so that you can attach the scales without excess fabric getting in the way, and secure with safety pins.

3 Start attaching the small scales at the hem in the centre front of the skirt (so that if there are any discrepancies, they will be at the centre back). Leaving a gap of 2–3 mm (1/8 in.) between the scales, stitch each scale individually by hand and secure the thread at the back. Do not continue the thread from one scale to the next or it will prevent the Spandex from stretching, which is necessary for movement and fit.

4 About two-thirds of the way up the skirt, change to the larger-sized scales (this is optional – you can use the same size of scale throughout if you wish). When you start a new row, place the first scale above and in between the first two scales of the previous row to

stagger them in a 'brick' pattern and overlap each row of scales by placing the upper scales about one-third of the way down the scales in the row below.

5 As the skirt widens, you will need to adjust the gaps to fit in the extra scales needed in the longer rows, but this is gradual, so there should not be a big jump. Keep rolling the skirt back until you reach the waist and finish. You can also start carefully rolling up the scaled areas to keep them out of the way, so you have a rolled-up piece on either side of the area you are sewing.

Bolero top

1 Lay the bolero pattern over the leotard shoulder straps to make sure they are not wider. It will look untidy if the leotard straps poke out from underneath. Cut the bolero shoulder straps wider than the pattern if necessary or fold the leotard shoulder straps under and sew them to make them narrower.

2 Cut out one bodice front and two bodice backs if using Spandex, and two bodice fronts and four bodice backs if using Lycra.

3 If you are using Lycra, pin the pieces together, so that the bolero has two layers. With right sides together,

using a stretch stitch, machine stitch around the neckline, hem and one centre back. Clip the curved seam and turn right side out. Tack around both layers of the armholes, along the bodice hem and down the remaining centre back, so that the fabric cannot slide around.

4 If you are using Spandex, with right sides together, using a stretch stitch, machine stitch the fronts to the backs along the shoulder and side seams, leaving the centre backs open.

5 Machine stitch Velcro at the centre back. Turn back the right-hand side and sew it in place.

6 Decorate the bolero top with a mixture of sequins and crystals sewn on individually by hand. Do not conect the threads between sequins, as this will inhibit the stretch.

Tail fin frill

1 If you are using polythene bags for the tail fin frill, rather than a polythene sheet, cut the sides and open the bags out.

2 Pin the 'seaweed' patterns on the polythene (it is slippery and will need to be well pinned). Draw around the outline with a fine-tipped marker pen. Cut two or more at a time if you can, cutting just inside the shapes to get rid of the pen lines. You will need to cut four of each size.

3 Remove the paper pattern and make one cut from the outside of each circle, as marked on the pattern, to the inner circle, enabling it to open up. Lay out four circles in descending and then four in ascending order of size. Overlap one cut edge on the same cut edge on another circle, pin the circles together, and straight stitch on the machine. Make sure you backstitch all the seams. Alternatively, join the circles with strips of clear adhesive tape.

4 Continue in this way, joining one circle to another, until the tail fin frill is complete, leaving the centre back (the longest part) open.

5 Machine two parallel rows of gathering stitching along the inside curves. Pull up the back threads from both ends to gather the frill to the length of the outside edge of the basque.

6 Tie off the ends to secure and finish with a blob of glue to make sure that the knots do not come undone.

Assembling the tail fin

1 Cut the basque from Spandex. Machine two rows of gathering stitches (see page 13) along the inside (shorter) edge, but do not gather up just yet.

2 Pin the gathered edge of the tail fin frill to the outside edge of the Spandex basque, then overlap the gathered edge of the tail fin and pin together. Using a wide but short zigzag stitch, join the tail fin frill to the basque, making sure that the smallest circles are at the centre.

3 Pin the inside (gathered) edge of the basque to the inside of the hem of the skirt. Check the length on the child; it should be ankle length at the front and long, like a train, at the back.

4 Attach the basque to the base of the skirt, if possible using a fine (not micro) tagging gun, tagging every 1 cm (½ in.) and keeping both tag ends on the outside. Alternatively, hand stitch the basque in place, taking care not to reduce the hem. There is no need to fasten the centre back of the tail fin; it can be left permanently open.

Useful Tip

When attaching the basque, do not pull the stitches too tightly or it may restrict the stretch in the Spandex.

Attaching the skirt to the leotard

1 Fit the assembled skirt and tail fin frill on the child, with the child wearing the leotard, and mark in tailor's chalk or in dots with a fine marker pen where the top of the skirt should be sewn to the leotard. Do not turn the top edge of the skirt over. The waist should be a dropped waist, but not a full-on hipster.

2 Pin together, then herringbone stitch the skirt to the leotard (see page 11). Herringbone stitch will retain the stretch in both garments making it possible to shimmy into, even if it is a snug fit. Finally, sew a few scales and sequins over the join.

3 Pin, then herringbone stitch the bolero to the leotard, stitching only at the front of the bolero.

Seaweed boa

1 Using a fine-tipped marker pen, on the flat side of the bubble wrap, mark out approx. 19 'seaweed' shapes, depending on how long you want the boa to be. Cut out, cutting just inside the marked lines to remove the ink.

2 Cut a straight line from the outside to the inside circle of each seaweed piece, as marked on the pattern. Open out, pin the pieces together, and join by overlapping and machining one cut edge over the next. Continue until you have one long strip of seaweed.

3 Machine two rows of gathering stitching along the inside edge, in exactly the same way as for the tail fin frill. Pull up the back threads and secure with blobs of glue. Each seaweed shape should be gathered to approx. 16 cm (6¼ in.).

Useful Tip

Place the bubble wrap bubble side down in the machine. The bubble wrap may stick a little on the first row of gathering stitches, but just pull it gently through. The second row is easier, as the bubbles will have been popped by the needle.

4 Join the two ends of the seaweed together to form a big circle. Divide the circle in two, but not evenly: one side should be longer than the other so that it hangs down at the back. Pin safety pins approx. 32 cm (12½ in.) in from each end, pinning both lengths together.

5 To make wrist straps, take two pieces of millinery elastic, slightly shorter than the circumference of the child's wrist. Knot the loose ends together to form a loop. Colour the elastic with a blue or green marker pen if you wish; elastic does not dye well. Stitch the elastic loops around the points where the safety pins are, catching both lengths of boa together.

6 Check that the boa does not hang any lower than mid-calf on the child, so she can't trip up over it.

7 For an added optional detail, make a couple of extra pieces of gathered clear polythene the same size as the bolero neckline trim, and stitch one onto each wrist loop.

8 For a magical underwater finish, tag cup sequins, concave side facing out, in between the bubbles, scattering them at random all over both sides of the boa, using a micro tagging gun. If you do not possess a tagging gun, you can sew the sequins on. Glue is not effective on polythene, but tiny pieces of double-sided tape would work well (if you have the patience!).

Shoes

Translucent jelly shoes are ideal. Alternatively, use simple ballet flats or pumps.

sharp-toothed shark

With his mouth full of razor-sharp, pointed teeth, this monster of the deep's bite is definitely worse than his bark! But don't worry, with these soft foam gnashers, he won't rival Jaws, other than being very, very frightening to all who encounter him.

You will need

FOR THE BODY SUIT AND SPATS

Grey fleece fabric
Black cotton quilted lining fabric, preferably with cotton on both sides
Chunky zip to fit
Medium-sized black hook-and-eye fastening for back of neck
5 x 2-cm (¾-in.) black buttons
Black elastic, 2.5 cm (1 in.) wide, for stirrups

FOR THE HEAD

Bright pink or black Fun Foam for head shell
Grey fleece for head covering
Bright pink stretch velvet, Spandex or Lycra for lips
Approx. 1 m (1 yd) fine black millinery elastic for the loops to join head to body
White Fun Foam for teeth and fins
2 polystyrene balls, 4 cm (1½ in.) in diameter, for eyes
Black acrylic paint or marker pen

GENERAL EQUIPMENT

Pins
Tape measure
Fabric scissors
Craft knife and cutting mat
Contact adhesive
Plastic sheet or opened-out bin bags to protect work surface
PVA adhesive

Body

1 Cut out the front and back body pieces from grey fleece and quilted lining fabric. Pin, then tack the grey fleece fabric and the corresponding quilted lining pieces together. If your quilted lining fabric has cotton on only one side, then the two fabrics should be placed

wrong sides together, so that the cotton side will be next to the child's skin.

2 With right sides together, machine stitch the two back pieces together, leaving an opening in the centre back for the zip, as marked on the pattern. Insert the zip (see page 12).

3 With right sides together, machine stitch the two front pieces together along the centre front. Machine stitch the front to the back along the side seams.

Arms and neck

1 Cut the sleeves from grey fleece and from quilted lining fabric. Pin, then tack the grey fleece fabric and the corresponding quilted lining pieces together. Cut the hand facings from grey fleece.

2 With right sides together, machine stitch the underarm seams, leaving openings for the thumb and hand as indicated on the pattern. Turn the sleeves right side out. With right

sides together, machine stitch the facings to the ends of the sleeves. Turn the facings to the inside of the sleeves and hand stitch in place.

3 With right sides together, aligning the underarm seams with

the body suit side seams, pin the sleeves into the body. Machine stitch. Clip the curved seams.

4 Cut a strip of grey fleece and bind the neckline (see page 18).

5 Stitch a hook-and-eye fastening at the back of the neck above the zip.

Spats

1 Before you cut out the spats, check the patterns against the shoes that are going to be worn underneath and adjust if necessary.

2 Cut eight uppers (four left and four right) from fleece, and four uppers (two left and two right) from quilted lining fabric. Tack the lining pieces to the wrong side of four of the fleece pieces. Place the lined and unlined pieces right sides together in pairs, and

machine stitch the centre seam. Then machine stitch all around the outer edges, leaving a gap where it meets the leg. Notch the seams. Turn right side out.

3 Hem the back of the leg to the required length at the child's heel. Machine or hand stitch the ankle part of the spats to the front half of the legs, stopping at the side seams.

4 Hand stitch one or two lengths of elastic across the bottom of the spats to make stirrups.

Head

1 Using a craft knife on a cutting mat, cut out the head shell pieces from Fun Foam.

2 Following the manufacturer's instructions and working in a well ventilated area, coat the seams with contact adhesive (see page 8) and leave until touch dry. Join both front head pieces and both back head pieces together edge to edge along the centre front and centre back seams, then join the side seams.

3 Cut out the head-covering pieces from grey fleece.

4 With right sides together, using a stretch stitch, machine stitch the front and back head pieces together, aligning the seams at the point of the nose. (Although it is not a stretch fabric, fleece does have a lot of give in it.)

5 Cut out the lips from bright pink stretch velvet, Lycra or fleece, then pin them, right sides together, to the mouth opening. Machine stitch the lips to the fleece around the mouth opening, using a stretch stitch.

Materials

Fun foam is the most suitable material for making the head shell, as it is very light, easy to cut and forms well to the curves. Bright pink or black would be good as an interior to the head, and you will need white for the teeth. The fins can be any colour, as they are covered.

Useful Tip

Make sure that the lips are not over-stretched inside the mouth or they will disappear completely.

6 Clip the curved seams and the point on the head covering. Take five lengths of millinery elastic and knot the loose ends of each one together to form a loop. The loops will hook around buttons on the suit to keep the head on. Sew the loops into position, as indicated on the pattern.

7 Pull the covering inside out over the foam head to check the fit, aligning the seams on the Fun Foam and the fleece. If it is too loose, pin out any excess only in the centre back seam if possible, then remove the covering and machine as marked. If it is too tight, release the centre back seam and pin where the adjusted seam line needs to be.

8 Turn the covering right side out and pull it over the head shell. Turn the lips fabric to the inside of the mouth, stretch and pin, using dressmaking pins in the same way that you would use a map pin, to get the tension right. Using contact adhesive or hot or cool melt glue, stick the inside of the lips to the inside of the head, bit by bit, removing the pins as you go.

9 Turn the excess fabric at the base of the head covering to the inside of the head shell, taking care not to overstretch it or the elastic loops may not reach the buttons on the costume. Once it is in position with the seams aligned correctly and with no lumps or tucks anywhere, glue the fleece into the head shell.

10 Fit the body suit and head on the child. On the body suit, mark the position of the buttons that will hold the head in place, making sure they align with the elastic loops attached in Step 6. Sew on the buttons.

Teeth

1 Cut out the teeth from white Fun Foam. The pattern is in two halves, so you will need to make a right and a left. The teeth can easily be shaped with scissors to make them look sharp.

2 Using contact adhesive or hot glue, fix the teeth sections to the inside of the head on either side of the mouth opening, over the seam allowance of the lips fabric.

Fins

1 Cut out two fins from white Fun Foam – one for the head and one for the body. Cut out the fin covers from grey fleece.

2 With right sides together, pin the fin covers together and, using a stretch stitch, machine stitch along two sides, leaving the base open. Trim the points of the seams. Turn right side out, slip the covers over the foam fins, and smooth out the seams.

3 Turn the seam allowances under the Fun Foam bases and pin the fins to the fleece on the head and body, making the fleece taut. Slipstitch around the fleece edge at the base of the fins to form a very firm join, catching the quilted lining on the body as you sew to stop the fins from wobbling.

Eyes

1 Colour the polystyrene balls black, using black acrylic paint or a black marker pen. (Test that the pen does not melt the polystyrene.)

2 Using a craft knife on a cutting mat, carefully cut a small slice off one edge of each ball to form a glueing surface. Discard the small slices.

3 Glue the eyes to the head with PVA adhesive. (Polystyrene can melt with most glues.)

Useful Tip

Sew the fin on the body right alongside the zip to keep it as stable as possible. It is important that this join is firm, as it is more likely to wobble than the fin on the head.

Useful Tip

The size of the eyes depends on the size of the costume you are making. Beady eyes are good! Craft and art shops sell bags of different-sized polystyrene balls quite cheaply, so you can choose your size. Our shark has eyes that are 4 cm (1½ in.) in diameter.

Ping-pong balls can make great eyes, but they are hollow so they would be difficult to attach in this instance.

Suppliers

UK RESOURCES

GENERAL ART & CRAFTS STORES

Projects in this book use general crafts materials, ranging from adhesive, scissors, pliers and marker pens to more specialised products such as acrylic paints, brushes, poly board, Fun Foam or Funky Foam, polystyrene balls and beads. For details of your local crafts stores, search online or check your telephone directory.

John Lewis
Stores nationwide
0845 604 9049
www.johnlewis.com

HobbyCraft
35 stores nationwide
0800 027 2387
www.hobbycraft.co.uk

Fred Aldous
37 Lever Street
Manchester, M1 1LW
0161 236 4224
www.fredaldous.co.uk
Good online craft store.

HABERDASHERY, FABRIC & BEAD SUPPLIERS

Local markets are a good source for haberdashery and fabrics and are often less expensive than art and craft shops.

Abakhan Fabrics
111–115 Oldham Street
Manchester, M4 1LN
0161 839 3229

Beadworks
21a Tower Street
Covent Garden
London, WC2H 9NS
020 7240 0931
Mail order: 020 8553 3240

Creative Beadcraft
Mail order: 01494 778 818
www.creativebeadcraft.co.uk

MacCulloch & Wallis
26 Dering Street
London, W1S 1AT
020 7629 0311
www.macculloch-wallis.co.uk

Rainbow Textiles
98 The Broadway
Southall, UB1 1QF
020 8574 1494

The Fancy Silk Store
27 Moat Lane
Birmingham, B5 5BD
0121 643 7356
www.fancysilkstore.co.uk

GENERAL DIY STORES

Scissors, adhesives, pliers, dyes, tapes, small tools and glue guns are readily available from DIY and hardware stores and are often cheaper than craft shops. These stores have branches nationwide.

B&Q
0845 609 6688
www.diy.com

Homebase
0845 077 8888
www.homebase.co.uk

Robert Dyas
0845 450 3004
www.robertdyas.co.uk

US RESOURCES

MISCELLANEOUS

Don't forget to try charity shops, jumble sales, pound shops and online auction sites, such as ebay.

Claire's Accessories
Branches nationwide
www.claires.com

Hairaisers Wigs
9–11 Sunbeam Road
London, NW10 6JP
020 8965 2500
www.hairaisers.com

Pentonville Rubber
104/106 Pentonville Road
London, N1 9JB
0207 837 7553
www.pentonvillerubber.co.uk
Foam and rubber supplier.

www.seatweavingsupplies.co.uk
Centre cane for butterfly wings.

www.kiteshop.co.uk
Fibreglass rods for butterfly wings.

Dharma Trading
1604 4th Street
San Rafael, CA 94901
800-842-5227
www.dharmatrading.com
Dyes, resists, and fabric paints.

Hobby Lobby
Over 400 branches nationwide
www.hobbylobby.com

Metalliferous
34 West 46th Street
New York, NY 10036
212-944-0909
www.metalliferous.com
Metal, findings, and bead supplies.

Michaels
Branches nationwide
800-642-4235
www.michaels.com

Purl Patchwork
147 Sullivan Street
New York, NY 10012
212-420-8798
www.purlsoho.com
Fabrics and materials

Reprodepot Fabric
www.reprodepot.com

index

Acknowledgements

I would particularly like to thank the following costume makers for their help, advice and generosity with the making of this book: my sister Lal d'Abo, Niki Lyons, Day Murch and Sten Vollmuller. Special thanks also to Hannah Summers for her imaginative styling, Marianne Elgaard Bendsten for her infectious enthusiasm and hard work on this project, and to Holly Dobson for her invaluable assistance 'on set'.

A big thank you to costume makers Ginette Hughes, Beth Madden, Rachel Frost, Äsa Skold, Eve Healy Cathcart and Gaia Facchini.

And to the publisher and editors, Katie Cowan, Miriam Hyslop and Michelle Lo, thank you for making this book a reality. To Becky Maynes for her inspired photography, Barbara Zuniga for her design and a special thank you to Sarah Hoggett for making sense of my rambling text!

And lastly thank you to all our lovely models Antoinette, Biba, Dexter, Ella, Jade, James, Oriana, Presley, Raz, Ruby and Rudy who brought the costumes to life.

Picture credits

Photography by Rebecca Maynes

PatternMaker Software

Project Coordinator, Documentation: Kim Nish
PatternMaker Team: Tamara Vlasuk, Catherine Mehlhaff, Pat McDaniel, Taylor Fabian, Brian Pickrell, Gary Pickrell, Lane Holdcroft and a special thanks to Jon Parshall and James Ramey at Codeweavers as well as all the folks at FedEx Kinkos in Fairfield, CA for pattern help.

About the author

Vin Burnham is an award-winning costume designer who started as a costume maker at the Royal Opera House, Covent Garden. She went on to work for Jim Henson's Creature Shop before moving into TV and film, creating Aslan the Lion for The BBC's Chronicles of Narnia, and the Batsuit for Tim Burton's Batman and Batman Returns. More recent design credits include The BBC's Wind in the Willows starring Matt Lucas and Bob Hoskins for which she received a Royal Television Society nomination. She acted as special costume consultant for the BBG/Ragdoll's pre-school series In the Night Garden and designed the costumes for ZingZillas. Vin's costumes for TV Commercials include BMW, Volvo, IBM, Lloyds Bank, Heinz and McVities Penguin Biscuits which won Best Costume for the British Advertising Awards 2003. She has designed and made costumes for, amongst others, Sean Connery, Michelle Pfeiffer, Heather Graham, Gary Oldman, Peter O'Toole, Imelda Staunton, Matt LeBlanc, Drew Barrymore, Danny DeVito, Billy Zane, Robert Carlyle and Terence Stamp.

Love crafts?

Crafters, keep updated on all exciting craft news from Collins & Brown. Email lovecrafts@anovabooks.com to register for free email alerts and author events.